SUPPORT OUR HEALING

Support Our Healing: Helping Young People with Trauma, PTSD, Anxiety, Depression and Medical Needs. A Guide for Health Professionals, Educators and Caregivers – From a Teen Who Lives It

Published by Our Pixie Friends Pty Ltd 2025, Queensland, Australia
www.ourpixiefriends.com

Copyright © 2025 Our Magical Friends Holdings Pty Ltd ATF Our Magical Friends Trust

All rights reserved.

The moral right of the author, Siobhan Wilson, to be identified as the author of this work has been asserted.

No part of this book may be reproduced, stored in a retrieval system, or transmitted in any form or by any means, electronic, mechanical, photocopying, recording or otherwise, without prior written permission from the publisher. It may not be shared or transmitted for public or private use. 'Fair use' of brief quotations embodied in the text may be used with credit to the author.

Book Design by Siobhan Wilson and The Enever Group

ISBN Printed Version: 978-0-6488288-7-7
ISBN for e-book version: 978-0-6488288-6-0

Disclaimer
Our Magical Friends Holdings Pty Ltd, Our Pixie Friends Pty Ltd, and the author, Siobhan Wilson, make no representation and give no warranties as to the accuracy or otherwise of any information contained within this resource. We do not accept any responsibility for any omissions, errors or inaccuracies of any information, text, stories, strategies or anything else whatsoever and will not be held liable for any loss, damage or harm arising as a result of the use of this text. Users are advised to seek medical advice from qualified medical practitioners or mental health professionals and not to rely on, act or refrain from acting on medical advice due to any interpretation of text or anything else whatsoever contained within this book.

Readers are advised to read the Content Warning and Legal Disclaimer contained within the book. By reading this book, you acknowledge and accept that any actions you take based on its content are undertaken solely at your own risk, and you understand that you are advised to seek your own medical and professional advice.

Not recommended for readers under 18.

Support Our Healing

Siobhan Wilson

Dedicated to my incredible mum.
None of the good in my life would have happened
without you.
Thank you for being my biggest support—
in every room, at every test, through every tear.
I love you.
I hope you know how much it means to me
when you're there.
You are such a big part of all the
moments that matter.
I love you.

Disclaimer

Content Warning

This publication contains references to topics that may be distressing or triggering for some readers. These include, but are not limited to: self-harm, depression, suicide, family violence, alcoholism, homelessness and death. These subjects are presented as part of the author's lived experience and are included to promote understanding and awareness. Reader discretion is advised, especially for any individuals who may be sensitive to these themes.

Due to the nature of content, this book is recommended for 18+.

If you are in crisis or require emotional support, please seek help from a qualified professional or contact a crisis service in your area. In Australia, support is available from:

Lifeline Australia – 13 11 14
Kids Helpline – 1800 55 1800
Beyond Blue – 1300 22 4636

Legal Disclaimer

This autobiography reflects the personal experiences, views, and reflections of Siobhan Wilson. It includes discussion of various strategies and approaches the author found helpful and unhelpful during her developmental years while living with severe medical and mental health trauma. Any strategies, reflections, or suggestions described are not guaranteed to be suitable or effective for other individuals. **Readers must not use any part of this book as a basis for self-diagnosis, or as a reason to delay, disregard, or avoid seeking professional advice.**

This publication is provided for informational purposes only and does not constitute medical, psychological, psychiatric, therapeutic, or professional advice. The contents are not intended to be a substitute for professional care or treatment. To the fullest extent permitted by applicable law, including the laws of Australia, the author, publisher, and any associated entities disclaim all liability for any loss, injury, claim, damage, or adverse consequence arising from the use or misuse of any information contained in this publication.

By reading this book, you acknowledge that it is recommended for 18+, accept that any actions you take based on its content are undertaken solely at your own risk, and understand that you are advised to seek your own medical and professional advice.

Contents

Dedication	iv
Disclaimer	v
A Note Before You Begin	x
Nicu Warrior to Youth Advocate	xiii

SECTION ONE	1
Physical Health	2
1 Eczema: Beneath My Skin	3
2 Asthma: Breathing Battles	11
3 Allergies and Anaphylaxis: Threats All Around	20
4 Epileptiform Brainwaves: What Am I Doing?	30
5 Chronic Pain: The Pain You Cannot See	38
6 Bowel/Bladder Dysfunction: Body Embarrassment	44
7 The Magic of Appointments	51
Mental Health	58
8 Anxiety: The Fear of 'What If?'	59
9 PTSD and OCD: Living in Survival Mode	70
10 Grief: Loss in Many Forms	78
11 Depression: When the World Feels Too Much	86

12	Suicidal Thoughts: The Shame of Needing Help	92
13	Body Image and EDNOS	102
SECTION TWO		110
Neurodiversity		111
14	What Is NVLD? – A Timeline of Understanding	112
15	NVLD: What it Feels Like	118
16	Social Communication: Misunderstanding People	126
17	Executive Function: Not Getting it Right	133
18	Visual-Spatial: Where in the World is Siobhan?!	140
19	Sensory Processing: When It's All Too Much	151
20	Literal Interpretation: What Did You Mean?	159
SECTION THREE		164
Trauma		165
21	Social and Family Trauma: Where's Home?	166
22	Medical Trauma: The Sharp Sting	172
23	Owning My Body: Power Imbalance	182
24	Lack of Awareness In Our Community	190
SECTION FOUR		195
Strategies For Age Groups		196
25	Strategies for Ages 0-2	197
26	Strategies for Ages 2-5	202
27	Strategies for Ages 5–10	211
28	Strategies for Ages 10–16	220
Strategies for Neurodiversity		229
29	I Want to Talk: Social Communication Strategies	230
30	Calm During Storms: Regulation Strategies	234

31	Help Me: Executive Function Strategies	240
32	Look Over Here: Focus and Attention Strategies	245
33	Jam Roll: Sensory and Motor Planning Strategies	249
34	Navigating the World: Visual-Spatial Strategies	253
35	Learning Differently: Academic Strategies	260
	SECTION FIVE	265
	Additional Material and Resources	266
36	When God Was the Only Light Left	267
37	Breathing and Support	270
38	From Idea to Impact – Our Pixie Friends	277

Final Words — 282
Acknowledgements — 283
References — 289

A Note Before You Begin

Dear Reader,

You picked up this book. You've started reading. That tells me one of two things:

1. You're in the store deciding whether or not to buy this book - in which case, please do. You might learn a lot!
2. You're in a safe, comfy space, book in hand, ready to learn—and that says a lot about you. You *care*. About your kids, your clients, your students—whoever you're here for. You're the kind of person who goes the extra mile. You know there's always more to learn, and you're open to listening—*really* listening—to a child's perspective.

You get that textbooks give neat little examples, but real life? It's messy. You're here for the grey areas. You want to understand trauma that doesn't always fit the script. You want to help kids heal. You want to make it okay to be un'normal'.

If that's you, then from the bottom of my heart—*thank you*. Thank you for caring. Thank you for being open to other perspectives. I hope you'll believe me when I say some of my experiences went way off the rails from what the books said. A lot of the kids I meet are the same. Healing takes love, patience, and understanding—and people like you. So again, thank you.

How to Read This Book

This book tells the story of my life—my challenges, my triumphs, my fears, and my hopes. It's been written from my heart, and I've tried to be as honest and real as possible. Some parts are raw and emotional, because life isn't always easy, but I've also included things that helped me. I want this book to be useful—not just a story, but something that makes a difference. I want people to gain a better understanding of children and ways they can support them. If I can have on impact on even one life, it will have been worth it.

You can read the whole book from start to finish. In fact, I recommend doing this first, because it helps you see the full picture, the insights and strategies that you might find helpful, even in chapters you didn't think would apply. However, I understand that sometimes you're strapped for time or just need a quick reference. If that's the case, you can also search for a chapter that's relevant to your situation. If you have a child with eczema or who is struggling with suicidal thoughts, you might want to go straight to those chapters. If you're working with a child of a certain age, the age-based strategy sections might be most helpful. If you're supporting a child with neurodiversity, you might like to read the sections on social communication, executive function, sensory processing, or literal thinking.

While reading, you might come across something that feels confronting or reminds you of something hard from your own life. If that happens, please take care of yourself. It's okay to take a break. You can put the book down and come back later. You can skip chapters that feel too much. This book is here to help, not hurt, so be kind to yourself as you read. If it ever feels like it's getting too much, please reach out for professional support. You are not alone. At the back of the book, there's a section called *Breathing and Support* which includes strategies to help you calm down and feel more grounded in the moment. At the end of the book, you'll also find a page with links to other helpful resources. These are there in case you want more support, more ideas, or just a place to start exploring more.

Please read this book in the way that works best for you. There's no right or wrong way. Just take what you need, when you need it.

Your trauma advocate,

Siobhan

Nicu Warrior to Youth Advocate

I've been fighting since the day I was born.

My life began in a hospital—hooked up to machines, struggling to breathe, needing to be resuscitated multiple times a day. At just six weeks old, I had open heart surgery. That was only the beginning of a long list of medical challenges I would face. One nurse told Mum, "Don't you wake her. She's a feisty baby!" That tiny moment stuck because that feistiness, that will to keep going, has followed me through everything that's happened since.

Growing up, I faced more medical challenges than many people will in a lifetime but I'm aware too, that I have been lucky in so many ways. There are thousands of children who face more difficult challenges than I do. This is my story, my journey and I tell it in the hopes it will help other children.

I've lived with chronic conditions and constant medical appointments. I've had epileptiform brainwaves, asthma, bowel and bladder dysfunction, anaphylaxis, heat-induced rashes, and infections resulting in allergic reactions to medications. I've been through scary procedures and emergency hospital visits more times than I can count. On top of all that, I've experienced sensory processing difficulties, nociplastic (nerve) pain, and trouble with things like balance, coordination, swallowing, and speaking. By age two, I was diagnosed with Generalised Anxiety Disorder. By six, I had PTSD. At nine, I was already dealing with depression and suicidal ideations because I just couldn't handle my life any more. At fifteen, the PTSD came back accompanied by OCD.

I wondered why I wasn't like other kids, why things felt so much harder, why I seemed to miss the things others just understood. I often asked, "Why am I not 'normal'?" "What's 'wrong' with me?" I eventually learned I have NVLD—Non-Verbal Learning Disorder, a form of neurodiversity. It helped explain some of the things I'd been experiencing for years, but it didn't make them go away.

That feeling of being different, of not being seen or understood, is what motivated me to create my company, *Our Pixie Friends,* when I was just six years old. I wanted other kids going through hard times to know they weren't alone. My dream was to create magical characters who could help children feel happy with who they are and encourage other kids to be kind and inclusive. I wanted to boost self-esteem, build resilience and develop friendship skills, thereby creating a culture of kindness.

Teachers told me, "Wait until you're in Year 9. That's when you can learn about business," but I didn't want to wait. I kept working on my website ideas, developing my characters and writing my stories. By ten, I had registered my first business. By twelve, I published my first book and launched my website.

Since then, I've written three children's picture books that help kids cope with life's challenges. *Sakaela the Sneezy Pixie Visits Amy* is about finding courage during scary medical procedures. *Zizzy the Wheezy Pixie Meets Moondrop* shares a story about asthma, hospital stays, chemotherapy, and the importance of kindness and inclusion. *Minsky the Meltdown Pixie Helps Tommy* focuses on managing anxiety in gentle, relatable ways. My fourth book should be released soon about Paizo the Peanut Allergy Pixie, who has anaphylaxis at his birthday.

I created an interactive website with a map of Sprizzletania, home to all Our Pixie Friends, where children can listen to character audio blogs about coping with medical conditions, upload their own stories and artwork, print activities at home, watch videos, and feel like they belong to a magical community. All of my merchandise is designed with purpose. I even developed my own range of soft, silent sensory fidgets because I couldn't stand the hard, clicky plastic ones. These calming tools are integrated with the pixie world too. Everything connects—the books, the characters, the website, the merchandise—because I wanted kids to feel part of something bigger, not just a diagnosis.

10% of all sales is donated to medical research and through *The Cozipal Project*, I've donated over 530 personalised gift packs to children experiencing trauma—kids facing homelessness, domestic violence, abuse, or medical challenges. These packs have been sponsored by generous community groups and businesses and have gone to children across Australia and even overseas to the U.K., U.S. and South Africa.

Sometimes I get to visit children in hospital or at home, dressed as a pixie, to read my books and brighten their day. I've done readings at schools, homeless shelters, and for children who've experienced domestic violence. For a year, I also ran a friendship group for children with special needs, offering a safe, welcoming space for play, connection, and creativity.

I'm often asked to present workshops on creativity, entrepreneurship, and leadership, especially for young people. I've had the opportunity to speak at conferences for educators, mental health professionals, and healthcare workers. I'm also a Youth Advocate for the Queensland Family and Child Commission, part of a youth advisory group for the Black Dog Institute and a regular consumer representative for Queensland Health, helping improve services for kids and teens. Being asked to contribute to these conversations is something I never take for granted. It's a real privilege to help others by sharing what I've lived through.

Along the way, I've been recognised with awards like Young Entrepreneur of the Year, Business of the Year, the Paul Harris Fellowship, and a literacy award for 'transforming lives through literacy'. These honours help to highlight the importance of giving young people a voice so together, we can create meaningful change.

This book isn't a 'trauma dump' or a list of achievements. It's not a perfect story. It's a real one. I still have bad days. I still carry the scars of medical trauma and mental health struggles. The process of writing this book has been a struggle as I have been forced to face multiple trauma triggers but I have found power in listening to the stories of others, and have been honoured to be asked to share my story, in the hope that it will help many others struggling with life's challenges.

This book is for anyone who wants to understand what it's really like to grow up with these struggles, and for anyone who wants to make things better for the children in their lives.

If you're a young person going through something hard, I want you to know:
You're not alone.

You're not broken.

There's nothing wrong with you.

There's nothing to fix.

People care about you even when it doesn't feel like it.

If you're a teacher, health worker, support worker, or parent, I hope what you read here gives you not just insight, but practical ways to help.

You don't have to be perfect to make a difference.

You just have to begin.

SECTION ONE

Physical Health

1

Eczema: Beneath My Skin

Eczema isn't just a skin condition. It's something that affects your whole life. From the outside, people see red, flaky skin or hands that look sore, but they don't realise how deeply it can impact how you feel, how you live, and how others treat you. I've lived with severe eczema since I was a baby, and it has shaped how I see the world and how the world sees me.

Growing up with eczema meant being left out. My eczema was all over my hands and most of my body. I was very lucky because it didn't affect my face much, but that didn't make it any easier. Little kids didn't notice it as much, but as I got older, I wasn't invited to birthday parties or play dates very often. Kids worried they would 'catch' it, so when they didn't hold my hand in line, I was in trouble for not holding hands with my partner. They thought it looked weird. Some even thought it was something to laugh at. I was told eczema was for life, and at that point, I thought that meant I'd be excluded for life too.

The social impact of eczema doesn't stop at missing out. Kids and even adults often make comments without thinking. I've been told, "Your hands look like my Grandma's," "You've got elephant skin," and "Is that nits or dandruff all through your hair?" because I also have eczema on my scalp. Those words stay with you. I've had strangers offer me Band-Aids because they thought I'd been hurt. Even Mum once said, "People must think you're being abused or neglected… your skin's so bad." She didn't mean to hurt me. She was just worried but it still made me feel like my skin was something scary to others. It made me feel like I was the problem.

Pain is a daily part of living in my skin. Sometimes, my hands hurt so badly I can't even close them into fists. It's too painful. Writing with a pencil hurts. Doing up buttons can be impossible some days. The skin tightens and cracks, and moving too much splits it open so it bleeds everywhere. It bleeds on my books, my clothes and my bed. Asking for help with basic things can be frustrating and embarrassing but often I have no choice. It takes away my independence in little, constant ways.

Trying to treat eczema has been just as hard as living with it. Doctors gave me wet wraps, ointments, and creams but none of it worked the way it was supposed to. What people didn't realise was that I was actually reacting to some of the treatments, like steroids, which only made my skin worse. Even products 'recommended by dermatologists' caused burning and stinging. No matter how hard I tried, I kept hearing the same advice: "You just need to moisturise more." I was already trying. I was trying everything. I wanted to get better. Nothing worked.

They also told us to try bleach baths which are meant to help reduce bacteria on the skin. Mum diluted the bleach more than they said to but it still burnt me. I had to go to the doctor afterwards, and they recommended switching to Condy's crystal baths instead. At first, we weren't told how much to use, so we tipped too much in and I came out of the bath a strange browny-yellow colour like I had just been given a really bad fake tan. That part was kind of funny and we giggled ... a lot! Mum had a great time trying to clean the bath afterwards, and we both laughed when we realised you only need a few tiny crystals, not a whole handful!

One of the hardest parts of treatment was the wet wraps. I was covered in paraffin, creams, and layers of wet wraps, then dry wraps. In winter, it was awful. Wet wraps become cold very quickly and they are uncomfortable. Coming out of a warm shower, only to brace for the sting of the creams was something I dreaded. It didn't matter if it was cold or hot outside: either way, the weather hurt. When it was hot, I would get heat-induced urticaria. When it was cold, my skin would dry out and split. The condition doesn't only limit what I can wear or how I feel: it also stops me from doing things other kids enjoy. After all, you can't really go anywhere when you are wrapped from head to toe with even your hands and feet covered in bandages like an Egyptian mummy!

I knew I had heat-induced urticaria. When I tried to play sport in summer, I would come out in red, itchy welts all over my neck, arms and legs. I would be sent up to the office to have antihistamines and ice packs, but sometimes it was so bad Mum would have to collect me from school so I could have a bath and put my wet wraps on. When I was about 8, I found out that temperature-induced urticaria meant I was impacted by the cold too.

One year, I carefully prepared my skin for a family holiday. I had been doing my wet wraps every night, and my creams every day as often as I remembered. My skin was the best it had ever been. I had no splits, no bleeding. I went to the pool and then the beach in Adelaide. I was so excited! But when I stepped into the cold water at the beach, my legs started to hurt. It was stinging and burning. I had to get out. My feet and legs up to my knees (where the water had touched) were covered in hives. Mum gave me antihistamines and took me to the doctor in case I had been stung by a marine animal, but they explained it was temperature-induced urticaria. That was the first time I realised the cold could hurt me just as much as the heat. I'd rather miss out on the beach than deal with the pain for hours afterward. Beach holidays are NOT fun.

It's hard not to let eczema take over your identity. Sometimes, the chlorine in pools can be bad for my skin as well as my allergic rhinitis, so along with the itchy hives, I start sneezing and my eyes water too. On top of it, I also deal with asthma, anaphylaxis, and chronic pain. All of these medical issues are tied together and can make me feel like I'm 'broken'. Eczema feeds into my anxiety. It adds to the fear of not being 'normal'. Of being different. Of being left out. It affects how I think about myself — not just how I look, but how I feel inside. It impacts my mental health and self-worth every single day.

The dermatologists tried Dupixent, an injection for eczema, but it caused joint pain. I had to stop it after only one treatment. It's upsetting because I'd hoped it would be the answer. I was holding onto hope that maybe it could help me go to the beach, exercise, or just manage my skin better without constantly fighting it. Now, it's just another "maybe" that probably won't work out and

I'm scared to try it again in case it makes the joint pain worse. Now they are talking about other drugs which have worse side effects than the eczema.

Even though eczema makes life hard, I've tried to take ownership of the things I can control. When I was little, Mum helped put my creams on, turning it into a fun routine by tickling me to make it feel less scary and singing songs like, "This is the way we put on the cream". But as I've gotten older, I've had to take more responsibility. It's hard to keep up, especially when you're already overwhelmed, but I try to manage it on my own.

Adolescence brings a new layer of challenges. I want to be independent. Sometimes I need to learn the hard way, to let my skin get bad, so I remember why I need to do the creams. It's all part of growing up with a condition like this. I don't want to rely on other people, but sometimes, I still need help. I want space to manage my eczema in my own way, but that doesn't mean I'm lazy or defiant. It means I'm trying to cope. Sometimes I just need a moment to feel like a normal teenager, without people commenting on my skin, asking if I've injured myself, or offering random advice. Even at business events with adults, people will come up to me and say what they think I should be doing to "fix" my skin. It's embarrassing. I want people to see me — the person beneath my skin.

Managing eczema also becomes harder when medical professionals give conflicting advice. One doctor says to use a particular moisturiser, and another says, "Don't use that — it's not good enough." Then I'm stuck in the middle, not knowing who to follow. I worry that if I pick the wrong one, they'll think I'm ignoring their treatment and won't help me any more. I wish they could see how hard it is to be the one stuck in the middle, especially as a kid or Teen.

There are other things that make daily life hard. Washing my hands stings. Walking on grass can trigger itching, rashes, or hives. Playing outside in the park might mean touching something that makes me break out. Pools and water parks are scary because the chlorine or salt water burns. Holidays that are fun for most kids can be painful and stressful for me. And when you add in how others treat you — the staring, the comments, the judgement — it can feel really lonely.

Still, I keep wondering what new treatments are on the horizon. Maybe there's something coming that will work — something that doesn't hurt, sting, or come with awful side effects. I like to believe that science is moving forward. Maybe one day I'll find something that finally helps. And maybe one day, other kids won't have to go through everything I have. I hold onto that hope. Hope that people will start to understand. Hope that my skin won't always rule my life. I'm learning how to manage it, but what would help most is for others to see past it. To see me.

Key Takeaways:

Trial-and-error is part of the process. Teach the child that every person has different skin. Some creams and sunscreens might burn, sting, or make things worse. Help children understand that it might take time to find what works for their unique skin. Be patient and validating as you work through the options.

Listen to the child, remain open-minded and believe them. What works for one child may not work for another. Some children react to steroids or common eczema treatments. If a child says the cream is burning or stinging, or that their skin feels worse after treatment, take them seriously. Don't dismiss them because their real-life experience matters more than what's "meant to" work in theory.

Stop treatments that cause pain. If a child says their skin is stinging or burning, let them wash it off. Don't say, "It will settle soon" or "That's normal." You're not the one feeling the pain and distress. Respect their voice.

Talk directly to the child, not just the parent. Include them in conversations about their skin. Let them feel seen and heard. This builds trust and helps them feel more in control of their own care.

Explain treatments in clear, simple words. Don't assume that the family will remember the final instructions if lots of different ideas have been discussed during the appointment. Write clear, step-by-step instructions. Include pictures (even quick stick figures or cartoon drawings) of the steps for the child to follow if they are too young to read.

Let the child choose how treatment happens. Offer choices like, "Do you want to put the cream on your arm, or do you want me to help?" Giving them a sense of control over little things can reduce anxiety and resistance.

Make treatment playful for younger children. Turn applying creams into a game. Sing songs like "This is the way we put on the cream," or use gentle tickles to reduce stress and make routines more manageable.

Recognise refusal as fear, not defiance. If a child doesn't want the cream, it might be because they're scared of pain. Acknowledge the fear instead of assuming they're being difficult.

Encourage growing independence, gently. As children grow, involve them in caring for their skin at their own pace. Don't rush it but support them as their confidence develops to manage their own care.

Avoid shaming or judgemental comments. Phrases like "That looks painful" or "Haven't you washed your hair?" can hurt deeply. Kids with eczema are often already doing their best. Instead, praise efforts. "I can see you put your moisturiser on today. Good on you."

Don't add pressure when advice conflicts. If multiple professionals give different instructions, it can be very confusing. Patients want to be healing but if they are being told different treatment plans, they don't know whose advice to follow and worry they will be labelled as 'uncooperative' or 'refusing treatment'.

See beyond the skin. Eczema affects friendships, self-esteem, and daily life. Don't just see the rash — see the whole child and the courage it takes to live beneath their skin.

2

Asthma: Breathing Battles

Asthma has been part of my life for as long as I can remember. Honestly, I can't even picture a time before it. Apparently, I started having symptoms before I was even two years old, but doctors aren't allowed to officially diagnose asthma until you're older. It's like some kind of weird rule they have. We didn't know how bad it could get but I'm one of the lucky ones. I know kids who have asthma far worse than mine.

I spent so much of my early life at doctors, in hospital emergency departments or doing everything possible to avoid being sent there. I had asthma a lot as a child, especially when I got sick. Any time I got any virus or infection, it would trigger my asthma and I would have it for weeks after the infection or virus had gone. One year, I had 15 chest infections. It got to the point where I had to have 12 puffs of Ventolin every two hours just to stay out of hospital. We had to keep the oral steroid, prednisone, in the fridge all the time. It wasn't always like that. It was only during those really bad periods. The rest of the time, I just had to keep on top of my preventers and use Ventolin when I needed it.

During the worst times, it took over everything. I couldn't sleep properly without worrying about the next dose or the next attack. It wasn't just my life that was disrupted—my whole family was often kept awake. Mum often had to get up around 3-4am to give me my puffer and when I went to Thunderbird Park to dig for geodes, I paid for it for a couple of weeks. (But it was worth it for the fun I had!)

Honestly, the part that scared me most wasn't even the breathing itself. It was the nebuliser. I was absolutely terrified of it. The machine made these strange, loud sounds that freaked me out. They would put this plastic mask over my face, and it smelt weird and 'chemical-y'. I felt like I was being suffocated before the medicine even started to work. I used to panic the second they brought the machine near me, and of course, panicking makes asthma worse, which just created this vicious cycle. It was supposed to help me but every time, I was more afraid of the machine than of the asthma itself. To me, it wasn't "safe." It felt like being trapped.

Even as I got older, asthma kept controlling much of my life. I remember there were many times I was too afraid to ask for my asthma puffers because I didn't want to be a burden. I didn't want to be the "difficult" one, the one who always needed something, the one who caused problems. I would sit there struggling to breathe, scared out of my mind, but still too scared to say anything because I didn't want people to get frustrated with me or roll their eyes or sigh. I didn't want to be seen as annoying. That fear of being a burden was sometimes even stronger than the fear of the asthma itself.

One afternoon, Mum came to collect me from after school care. I greeted her saying, "He...llo...Mum...my." I couldn't even say one word without needing to take a breath. Mum took me to the leader and they got my puffer. I had to have 6 puffs. After that, Mum helped me learn to ask for my puffer. We practised what words to say and what to do to get the leader's attention, then I practised it with the day care teacher too.

I finally got the confidence to ask when I needed help. I realised that staying silent wasn't going to keep me safe. It was just going to make things worse. I learned that my life mattered, and it was okay to speak up. It was okay to say, "I need my puffer," even if people didn't like it, even if it felt uncomfortable.

That's when I went to a Guide Camp—something that was supposed to be fun, right? Something 'normal' kids get to do. I had a written asthma plan with me. When I told the leaders I needed my puffer, they only let me have the standard 2 puffs, but that didn't help. I needed more. They didn't believe me. They thought I was exaggerating or being dramatic. It was bad. They refused to let me have more puffs. I can't even describe how scary that was—to be in the middle of an asthma attack, knowing exactly what I needed, and having people refuse to help. It was terrifying, frustrating, and honestly, humiliating. It made me feel invisible. Like my voice didn't matter. Like my life didn't matter.

As the afternoon wore on, I was desperate. After dinner, I was really struggling to breathe and it was getting worse. I didn't want to die at Guide Camp, but I didn't know what to do. I wanted Mum. I wanted to go home, but the Guide leader wouldn't let the other adult ring her. I walked through the dark to my cabin, where I lay on the bed alone and cried. I was so scared. Eventually one of the adults, the one who had initially wanted to ring Mum, came and found me. They finally rang Mum. It was 10pm. Mum had to collect me. She took me home and started giving me 12 puffs every 2 hours to avoid another hospital stay. When Mum spoke to the leaders at the next Guides meeting, it was apparent that they didn't understand the asthma plan. It was too complex for them to follow, with colour-coded sections they hadn't noticed and the details of what to do lost in the complex form. A simple step-by-step procedure needs to be clearly communicated on the forms.

Then I think about the time I had an asthma attack on a Noosa trip with the ASE Group—without Mum. The trip itself was so much fun. I was having the best time. However, I had eaten a little bit of colouring or something that triggered my asthma. At first, I tried to deal with it myself. I thought I could handle it, but nothing was working. I ended up having something like 30 puffs in one day. Thirty. I was so scared. I remember all the adults in the room. They asked if I needed an ambulance or to go to the hospital. I remember thinking, "I'm not going to make it. I'm not going to make it to the hospital or until the ambulance arrives." I could barely breathe. I remember panicking and thinking, "This is it."

Mum wasn't there, but they called her, and honestly, thank you to them. Thank you for taking it seriously. Mum instructed them to give me some antihistamines because dust can affect me too. They gave it to me and—wow—I started to feel better. I remember lying there, feeling so relieved, and also kind of amazed. I felt independent. I felt in control. And more than anything, I felt like the people around me would fight for me. They didn't dismiss me. They didn't make me feel dramatic or difficult. They listened to me. They actually listened—not just heard the words, but listened to what I was saying and what I needed. They didn't just rush to do whatever they were told in some random first aid course. They took control by giving me my medicine, but they did it *with* me, not *to* me. Afterwards, they kept checking on me throughout the night. 1am. 2am. 4am. They got up and made sure I was okay. They didn't just assume the danger had passed. They stayed alert. They stayed with me. They made sure I knew I wasn't alone. That made such a huge difference. I felt so safe. I knew that if I were to stop breathing in the middle of the night, I wouldn't be by myself. There would be someone right there, ready to help. I'll never forget how different that felt compared to the asthma attack at Guides. At Noosa, I was surrounded. At Guides, I was alone.

Asthma doesn't take breaks. It's not like I could just have a "normal" day without thinking about it. I also have to take preventers every single day. They are inhalers that help stop asthma from flaring up in the first place, but they only work if you take them consistently. And I'll be real—when you're a teen and you don't want Mum telling you what to do all the time, it's hard to remember every day. When you forget, suddenly you're back to square one—wheezing, coughing, scared.

Asthma is only one part of the story though. I also have anaphylaxis. And the two of them together?! That's when things get even scarier. After I had anaphylaxis three times in six months when I was four, every time I felt my chest tighten or I started to struggle to breathe, I wasn't just thinking "Oh, this is asthma." I'd immediately panic. "Wait—is this asthma? Or is this anaphylaxis? Am I about to die? Should I be getting my EpiPen? Should I be calling an ambulance?" The fear would take over so quickly. It wasn't just physical, it was mental. It was the panic, the uncertainty, the constant questioning. Is this the time something truly awful happens?

That's the thing people don't understand about living with both asthma and anaphylaxis. It's not just the breathing. It's the constant fear. The second-guessing. The "what ifs" that take over your brain. And when the panic kicks in, it makes the asthma worse. And when the asthma gets worse, it makes the panic worse. It's like being trapped in a loop you can't escape. Even when things are calm, I'm always on edge, waiting for the next time because I know there could always be a next time. I know it isn't "if", it's "when."

When you grow up like that, it changes you. I didn't just feel like a kid with asthma. I felt like a kid who was broken. Fragile. Like my body wasn't safe. Like I couldn't trust it. When adults didn't believe me or thought they knew what was best due to a little first aid course they had done, when they ignored my asthma plan, when they told me I was overreacting, it only made that feeling worse. It made me feel small and invisible. It felt like I didn't matter. You start to carry that with you—that sense that you have to fight to be heard. That you have to explain yourself over and over just to stay alive. It's exhausting. Asthma didn't just take my breath. It took my confidence. It took my sense of safety in the world.

Even now, years later, I still carry that fear sometimes. Every time I reach for my puffer, there's that split second of panic: "Is this just asthma? Or is this something worse?" I have to breathe through the fear before I can even breathe through the asthma. But I've learned things too. I've learned to stand up for myself, to say, "No, actually, I need this," even when people don't believe me. I've learned to take my preventers, to carry my medicine, to listen to my body. I've learned to tell the difference, most of the time, between asthma and panic and anaphylaxis.

But most of all, I've learned that asthma doesn't get to define who I am. It's part of my story, yes. But it's not all of me. It's made me brave in ways I never wanted to be. It's taught me resilience. It's taught me to speak up, even when my voice shakes, even when I'm scared, even when no one else seems to listen. That's what I want to tell other kids who live with asthma, or any condition like this. You are not weak. You are not a burden. You are not invisible. Your voice matters. Your safety matters. And you are braver than you even know.

Key Takeaways:

Believe the child, always. If a child says they are struggling to breathe or asks for their puffer, listen and act straight away. Don't assume they're exaggerating or dramatic even if they "look fine." Take every asthma concern seriously to reduce anxiety. Chest tightening is not something you can see from the outside.

Make asthma action plans simple and readable. Colour-coded forms and complex instructions can easily be missed. Rewrite the asthma plan into a simple step-by-step version that's easy for every adult, teacher, support worker and even the child (depending on their age) to follow, especially in emergencies.

Teach children the language to ask for help. Rehearse and role play what to say, who to go to, and how to speak up when they need their puffer. Help them build their confidence, so they learn to advocate for themselves.

Never shame a child for needing medication. Don't roll your eyes, sigh, or act annoyed. Children remember those reactions. It teaches them that needing help is a problem. It makes them feel they are a burden, an inconvenience. Instead, reassure them that asking for support is brave and important.

Address fear around medical equipment. If the child is scared of something like a nebuliser, acknowledge it. Don't force it without compassion. Help them understand the sounds, smells, and feelings involved. Let them know it's okay to be a bit scared, but reassure them it will be all right. Use role playing with toys to reduce the fear and help them learn what will happen.

Keep medicine accessible and updated. Make sure preventers are taken consistently and relievers are on hand, especially for camps, school playgrounds, or outings. Don't assume medicines left in the office will be accessible quickly. Never have emergency medicine stored in locked cupboards in school offices where it cannot be accessed quickly or only a couple of people know where the key is kept. Medical bags carried on or close to the child are best. I had a medical bag that the teacher reminded me to take with me whenever I left the room. I would hand it to the teacher on duty and collect it after lunch.

Respect that children know their own bodies. A child who lives with asthma every day usually knows when something is wrong. If they say the standard dose isn't enough, believe them and follow the plan, even if it goes beyond a "typical" first aid response.

Include children in their own care. Let the child be part of decision-making where possible. Give them a voice in how care is delivered. It helps build a sense of control and safety.

Don't delay medical help. If symptoms are getting worse, don't wait or argue. Call the parent or emergency services early. It's better to be safe than sorry.

Provide reassurance overnight. If a child has had a severe episode, continue monitoring through the night. Let them know someone will stay close and check on them. Feeling safe helps healing.

Create environments where kids feel safe speaking up. Whether at school, daycare, camp, or on trips, children should feel like their voice will be heard and respected. Check that all adults involved understand the child's medical needs and can provide both practical and emotional support. Help reduce the fear of being a 'burden', by reminding children that needing help does not make them annoying or weak. Affirm that they are important and valued.

Be aware of overlapping conditions. Asthma can feel even scarier when a child has had anaphylaxis. Understand that a child might be dealing with physical symptoms that are confusing and may indicate either asthma or anaphylaxis, but they may not know which. When in doubt, give adrenaline first.

Celebrate their bravery and resilience. Living with asthma isn't easy. Let children know how strong they are—not just for coping with symptoms, but for learning to speak up, to keep going, and to manage something that doesn't go away.

3

Allergies and Anaphylaxis: Threats All Around

Living with allergies isn't just about avoiding food or taking tablets sometimes. It's a constant part of my life. From the air I breathe to the food I eat, there are so many risks around me that could send my body into panic. I don't get to "forget" I have allergies. I always have to be aware. Some of my allergies cause discomfort and stress. Anaphylaxis could kill me. But no matter what type they are, they've shaped how I live, how I think, and how I feel every day.

My environmental allergies were the first ones I noticed. I'm allergic to grass, pollens, and dust mites. I break out in hives if I touch dusty or dirty things, or certain plants. My skin goes red and itchy, sometimes even painful. Every time the lawn gets mowed, I feel it straight away. My eyes swell up, get red and watery, and I sneeze over and over. My nose gets runny and it triggers my asthma. I have allergic rhinitis, and even going past someone mowing can trigger it. When we had an old car with no air conditioning, it was awful. I'd sit there itchy, with my eyes watering and sneezing my head off all the way to wherever we were going. Our new car is great! We can switch the air con to recirculate. At home, we shut all the windows and doors before the mower starts and I take my antihistamine to be ready.

The most serious of my allergies are my food allergies. I used to be allergic to dairy, eggs, peanuts, tree nuts, and shellfish. I passed oral food challenges and now I can eat eggs and prawns again, but I have to keep them in my diet regularly or I could lose tolerance. Now I'm mostly allergic to dairy and peanuts, but those two are enough to keep me on high alert every single day.

When I was four years old, I had three anaphylactic reactions in just six months. Each one was different. That's one of the scariest aspects. My body doesn't react the same way each time. People expect to see swollen eyes, lips and face, but I don't get that. I might just start coughing or have belly pain or feel dizzy. The first time it happened, I had a few bites of coconut rice and one prawn at a restaurant. I got itchy all over and my skin turned bright red. At first, Mum thought I'd touched something, so she took me to the bathroom to try to wash it off, but it didn't stop, so we headed home. It got worse. I started coughing. Mum told me to tell her if I had trouble breathing. A few seconds later, I did. She turned the car around and drove straight to the hospital. The doctor told Mum that if she had taken me home and just given me antihistamines, I would have died. That comment impacted all of us. Grandma started to cry. A few minutes later and I would have died. Later, we found out the restaurant had swapped coconut milk for regular milk without telling us.

The second time was when I had cabanossi. I was so excited! We had found dairy-free cheese and cabanossi that only said "may contain traces of dairy." We were told not to worry too much about "may contain" labels, so we went ahead and made pizza. I was so happy. But within just a few minutes of tasting the cabanossi, I had difficulty breathing. I had stridor—loud, rattly breathing—and it felt really scary. I felt like the world was closing in on me. Mum gave me the EpiPen, and Grandma called the ambulance straight away. The whole thing happened so quickly. Within ten minutes of my first bite, the ambulance was already nearly there. I didn't forgive Mum for giving me the EpiPen for a long time. In my mind, she had hurt me when I was scared. Now I know she saved my life... again.

The third time was during a holiday. We told every restaurant about my allergies, but we didn't know then how dangerous cross-contamination could be. I had an upset stomach and my skin started going a bit red. Mum wasn't sure if it was anaphylaxis or not, so she took me to the local hospital. They weren't sure either, so they kept me in to observe me. After about half an hour, my blood pressure was dropping and I said, "It feels like there's a tree in my chest.". That did it! They gave me adrenaline. Eight hours later (after we had exhausted just about every object in the ED playing 'I Spy') we thought I was okay, so I was sent home. However, in the morning, I woke up with a swollen face and had to go back to the hospital. It was a biphasic reaction—a second wave of symptoms. Anaphylaxis doesn't always stop after the first dose of adrenaline.

As I got older, I started realising just how scary anaphylaxis is. It's not just physical. It's emotionally and mentally draining too.

I live with that fear every day. At school, I was scared of peanut butter or dairy butter on sandwiches and spilled yoghurt. Some days, I couldn't even get out of the car because I was so afraid. I truly believed I could die at school and never see Mummy again. That's where my separation anxiety started. It wasn't just that I didn't want to be away from Mum. It was the terrifying belief that I might die and never get to say goodbye.

That kind of fear also made me feel alone. It's hard to make friends when sitting next to them feels like sitting beside a loaded gun. If a kid had butter, cheese, yoghurt or peanut butter, I didn't want to go near them. I started pulling away at lunchtime and sitting alone. It didn't help my social skills at all. I didn't know how to connect anymore. The risk was too high.

Another time, I had a really close call. We found a chocolate shop and I was really pleased to hear they had a dairy-free, nut-free chocolate. Mum asked which one it was and the lady showed her a chocolate in a display cabinet right next to all the other peanut and dairy ones. We explained that no, the risk of cross contamination there was so high, it wasn't safe. Then she showed us another chocolate in a different place, all individually wrapped ones. We asked again if it was dairy free and nut free and were reassured that yes, it was. But we still hadn't learned enough about checking every ingredient and relied on the shopkeeper's integrity. BIG mistake!

On the way home, I opened it up and had one lick. Almost immediately I said my tongue was itchy and started coughing. Mum was driving and asked me if I needed the EpiPen. I was about 8 or 9. I didn't know and there was nowhere to safely pull over, so we drove straight to the hospital. This time I was lucky. It was a moderate reaction, but fortunately not anaphylaxis. It turned out that the writing on the chocolate's logo that I had licked had contained traces of milk. That taught us to always, ALWAYS check every ingredient, every 'made on equipment that also processes', every 'may contain traces of' label every time. Not surprisingly, my food anxiety increased with each scary episode, and my trust in the food industry lessened.

At school camp, I was standing in line behind a child who suddenly vomited all over me. He had eaten milk in his cereal that morning, and my body reacted straight away. I broke out in hives and had to be given antihistamines, showered, and changed. I couldn't wear my shoes afterward, and because of that, I was excluded from fun camp activities I had really looked forward to, like the high ropes. More social exclusion. And now, a bigger fear of vomiting on top of it all.

And then came the worst one yet: a case of refractory anaphylaxis—anaphylaxis that doesn't respond to adrenaline.

It happened at a fancy restaurant gala dinner. We had filled in an allergy form prior to the event, but I still didn't trust them, so I asked about the food because it didn't look safe. The dietary waitress said it was dairy-free and nut-free. She checked about the mashed potato too and reassured me. I felt okay to eat. But soon after, my mouth felt itchy. My tummy hurt. I felt dizzy, hot and shaky. I stopped eating and switched to my own safe food, but the symptoms kept getting worse. At home, I ran to the toilet but was too late. I grabbed my Ventolin, but it didn't work. I tried to hide the reaction from Mum because I thought she might feel sick, but she found out and took over.

She ran for the EpiPen. Five minutes later, while on the phone to the ambulance, she gave me the second one. Still there was no improvement. I could barely breathe. My lips turned blue. I kept asking, "Am ... I ... going ... to ... die?" My chest was heaving. It was so painful. Mum kept saying, "I love you, darlin'," and stroking my head until I motioned for her to stop. Even now, I can't hear those words or have her touch my hair because it triggers flashbacks.

When the ambulance came, I was barely able to speak. They gave me oxygen and more adrenaline. Then more. Then more. They injected it every five minutes, put in a cannula, and gave me extra medication. I saw a bright light in the top corner of my room and had to fight to keep breathing. I remember feeling an internal tug-of-war. It was like a tug of war of life over death. I thought, "If I die, it will be easier." It was so hard to stay awake, but I knew it wasn't my time so I opened my eyes to do life again. It was such a hard choice.

The paramedics were arguing when one of them wanted to put adrenaline in the nebuliser. The other one said that would be breaking protocol and they wouldn't agree to that. I asked them if I was going to die and they just said they were doing everything they could, and they weren't allowed to let me die. I believed them. I clung to their words. Then I heard them begging the local hospital to take me because they were running out of adrenaline. They had their last syringe drawn up ready. One of them said, "I don't think she'll make it the extra 15 minutes to QCH." The hospital refused. I was too complex. I was absolutely terrified. I was sure this was it. I was going to die.

On the way to hospital, the adrenaline finally worked. I could breathe! I started shaking all over. My legs were purple and pale.

I joked about whether I'd set the record for the most adrenaline ever. They said, "Not even close." At the hospital, the doctors were shocked that this cheerful, chatty girl was the same patient who had needed so much adrenaline. So was Mum when she arrived. She had been so scared of what she would find since she had been unable to fit in the ambulance with the paramedics and the student.

In the hospital, I didn't feel safe. I was scared to eat the hospital breakfast. I only ate packaged fruit and juice. I realised I didn't trust food anymore—not even from people who were trying to help. Because it was Sunday and the hospital pharmacy was closed, I was released from hospital with NO EpiPens. I was terrified I could have a biphasic reaction, so Mum took me to the chemist immediately to have the new prescription filled.

When we investigated what had gone wrong, the closest we could come to an answer was that the manufacturer who had supplied the restaurant with the 'dairy-free' mashed potato admitted that it was made on the same equipment as the dairy mashed potato. I could no longer trust even the food manufacturers to be honest about allergens.

One of the hardest things is that not everyone understands how serious this is. People working in food places sometimes roll their eyes when I ask questions. What they don't realise is that their answers could decide if I live or die. Every person working in the food industry, from the person taking orders to the kitchen staff and waiters, needs to know the difference between a food preference, a mild allergy, and life-threatening anaphylaxis. They need proper training. But even more than that, they need to be kind and understanding when people question their safety practices. When

I ask if something is safe, I'm not being difficult. I'm trying really hard to protect myself, to stay alive.

I often get upset when people who have the luxury of eating out don't take that as a privilege and complain about the food. I would take that. I would eat that if I could. I'm craving eating out again, being able to live just a little bit normally - but I can't. I would LOVE to be in your situation having way too many options to choose from.

This is what life with anaphylaxis is really like. It's not a one-time emergency. It's trauma that repeats. It's waking up each day wondering if this will be your last day, and trying to live anyway.

Key Takeaways:

Take every reaction seriously. Don't wait for "classic" symptoms. Every child reacts differently, and symptoms can vary.

Act quickly, and don't second-guess yourself. If you suspect it could be anaphylaxis, use the EpiPen and call an ambulance. Don't wait. Jab first, ask questions later. Some reactions need more than one dose, and the earlier adrenaline is given, the better.

Respect the child's voice. Let them speak up, ask questions, and be part of their own safety. They know their body.

Teach others—teachers, family, carers. Make sure everyone around the child knows how to prevent, recognise, and respond to allergic reactions. If a child is at risk of anaphylaxis, regularly practise with a training device.

Check ingredients and all packaging labels every time. Companies can change ingredients any time. "May contain" labels can be dangerous. Check the entire package as sometimes warnings like 'made in a factory that also processes ..." may not be listed near the ingredients. Obtain medical advice from qualified practitioners about what's safe for you.

Help reduce environmental triggers. Close windows when mowing, keep dust down, and clean hands and surfaces after eating allergy foods. Wipe your child's hands before they play in parks or on equipment to help protect children with allergies who can react to things they touch.

Check ingredients on medications. Medications may contain hidden allergens. Check with pharmacists and manufacturers. Don't assume doctors or pharmacists know. Advocate for clearer labelling on medications. Understand that switching medication brands can be dangerous for kids with severe allergies as sometimes they react to the 'fillers', not just the drugs. I can't have penicillin in liquid forms for children, but I can have capsules opened up and put on a spoon.

Be aware that other products often contain allergens. Soaps, shampoos, toothpaste, creams and other beauty or personal care products may contain allergens. I saw a candle the other day that contained milk.

Train everyone in food service. From the front counter to the kitchen, everyone must understand the difference between food preferences and life-threatening allergies, and respond with kindness, not frustration.

Speak out when social media or other people make fun of serious reactions like anaphylaxis. Be an advocate for understanding to help build a culture of kindness. People with severe allergies do not deserve to be mocked.

Support emotional wellbeing. Living with allergies can cause anxiety, fear, trauma, and social isolation. Don't just treat the allergy—help the child feel emotionally safe too. They're not overreacting. They're managing risk and trying to survive. Be the calm, trusted adult they can count on.

4

Epileptiform Brainwaves: What Am I Doing?

Sometimes my brain feels scrambled. It's like someone has mixed up all my thoughts and everything feels jumbled, not just in the usual way of forgetting something or being tired, but in a deep, confusing, and scary way that's hard to put into words. I've had this since I was little. I have something called epileptiform brainwaves. Even now, those strange, scrambled moments still come, and they're hard to explain because the world around me doesn't just change in obvious ways. It shifts in quiet, eerie ways that make everything feel off.

When it happens, the colours around me get brighter, not in a nice, cheerful way, but in a way that feels too sharp and overwhelming. It's like the edges of everything glow a little too much. I don't feel grounded. It's like I'm not quite in the same world as everyone else. The strangest part is the thoughts. They don't feel normal. They come with this beat, this rhythm, almost like I can hear them but not with my ears. It's more like I can feel them echoing inside my head. There's a pulsing in my mind that doesn't make sense to anyone else, but it's very real to me. In those moments, I feel like my brain isn't mine anymore, and the fear that follows is huge.

During these episodes, I also find it almost impossible to think clearly. Even something as simple as adding 3 + 2 can feel impossible. My brain goes blank, or it feels like it's trying to move through fog. The harder I try to think, the more anxious I get, and the more anxious I get, the more scrambled everything becomes. It's like a loop I can't break out of. I get so frustrated with myself. I feel like I should be able to do something so simple, but I just can't. When that happens, sometimes the best thing I can do is stop. I need to walk away and do something completely different. That helps reset things a bit. It's not always easy, especially if I'm in a situation where walking away isn't possible, but I've learned that giving my brain a break is often the only way forward.

There was one time, when I was about eight or nine, that I got completely stuck on a maths problem. My working out was all over the page in the most random way. There was absolutely no logic to any of it. It looked like I was doing sums from another dimension. It was 'scrambled brain' in action. Twenty minutes later, I looked at the same question and solved it instantly.

Other times, instead of scrambling, my brain just seems to shut off. I tune out completely. I suddenly realise I've missed everything going on around me. I haven't heard what was said, or noticed what happened. It's like I just blank out of the world for a little while. These absences make learning really hard. When I used to go to school, I'd just miss things. I wouldn't even know what I'd missed until everyone else was moving on. There wasn't time to stop and say, "Wait, what just happened?" So I'd pretend I understood, even when I didn't. Now that I am homeschooled, it is different. If I tune out, I can say to Mum, "Um, I just missed whatever you said then. Can you say it again?" And she does. No one gets annoyed. I don't feel like a problem. I just get to catch up in a way that works for me. At school, it didn't feel like there was room for that. If you miss it, your learning goes into the abyss.

Sometimes I experience strange smells during an episode. One day, when I was younger, I was playing on the floor with my toys and started sniffing Mum's knee. I looked up at her and said "Mummy … your knee smells like vomit." Needless to say she felt extremely loved, seen and appreciated!

Even worse than the scrambled feeling or zoning out, though, was the fear of not being believed. When I was younger, the doctors decided I needed an EEG—a test where they attach wires all over your head to monitor your brain waves. I remember being really anxious about the goo they used to stick the wires on. I asked Mum again and again how I'd get it out of my hair. I didn't want to look weird or feel more different than I already did. Then I found out it would be an overnight EEG, and that made everything feel worse. I hated hospitals and I hated being away from home. Sleeping while being watched and monitored made me feel more like a science experiment than a person.

There were other things that made it even harder. Because of my allergies, I had to take all my own food to the hospital. That added to my anxiety because I was so scared of accidentally being given something unsafe. I worried constantly about food being cross-contaminated. It was just another reminder that my body didn't work like everyone else's, and that made everything feel more overwhelming.

My biggest fear wasn't the goo or the hospital stay or even the food. It was that they wouldn't find anything. That after all of that—the wires, the discomfort, the fear—they'd just say, "There's nothing wrong with you." I was terrified they'd think I was making it up. I didn't want to be the kid who wasted a bed or a test. I already felt different and broken. The idea that people might also see me as dishonest or dramatic made me feel even more alone. When they told me to press a button during the EEG if I felt something strange, it created a whole new layer of anxiety. I worried about whether what I felt counted. Was it real? Was it enough? What if I pressed it and they thought I was just making things up? Sometimes, I'd wait too long because I was sitting there questioning myself. Then I would panic that I'd missed the moment completely. Even something as small as pressing a button became something I second-guessed over and over.

That fear still creeps in now and then. Even though I know more about what epileptiform brainwaves are, and I have words to explain it now, the old doubts don't disappear. There's still a voice in the back of my mind that says, "What if no one believes you this time?" or "What if they think you're just being dramatic again?" That voice has been there for years. Even Mum, who tells me she believes me, can be hard to read. Because of my NVLD, I struggle with understanding if people mean what they say. I've learned that sometimes people smile while being sarcastic, or say nice things but don't really mean them. So when Mum says she believes me, a part of me wonders—does she truly believe me, or is she just trying to make me feel better?

The act of having an EEG also made me feel like there was something wrong with my brain. Not just something different—but wrong. Broken. I felt like I had to prove I was worth testing. And when the results came back, they didn't really explain anything to me. The neurologist told Mum that my results showed a "predisposition to right temporal lobe dysfunction." What does that even mean? Mum had no idea and the doctor didn't explain it, so she had to come home and try to research it herself. I still don't really know. It sounded fancy, but it didn't help me understand my brain or my experience. No one took the time to explain it in simple words I could understand.

That hurts too—not being included in the conversation about my own brain. People talked *about* me instead of *to* me. They used words I didn't understand, made decisions without explaining them, and expected me to just go along with it. I didn't feel like I was allowed to ask questions or admit that I didn't understand what was happening, so I stayed quiet. I put on my "I'm fine" mask and kept pretending everything was okay. I didn't want to be the kid who was too hard, too emotional, or too complicated. But pretending all the time is exhausting. Carrying that mask around made me feel even more alone. What I wish more than anything is that someone had told me, clearly and kindly, that I didn't have to prove my pain to be worthy of help.

I'm still learning that. It's taken me a long time to start believing that I'm not broken, that I'm not being dramatic, that I'm not a burden. I still get 'scrambled brain' days. I still get scared. But now I have words. I have people who listen, and most importantly, I'm learning to believe myself. Sometimes I still picture myself doing a task so clearly that I think I've already done it. Later, I try to prove to Mum that yes, I absolutely, definitely fed the guinea pigs... only to discover, nope. I just *imagined* myself doing it. Oops.

It turns out, even with scrambled brain, I can laugh. I can learn. I can connect. And I can be okay because I am not the problem. I am not too much. I'm just me. And that's enough.

Key takeaways:

Believe the child, even when you don't fully understand. If a child says their brain feels strange, scrambled, or off, trust them. Even if there's no obvious reason, their experience is still real. You don't need to fully understand it to support them.

Explain things in simple, clear language. Medical terms like "right temporal lobe dysfunction" don't mean much to a child or parent. Break it down in a way they can understand. Always check if they want more information.

Converse with the child. Listen to them patiently, giving them time to express what is happening for them. Include the child in conversations about their own body. Don't just talk about them as if they are not there.

Ensure they know what to expect and what is expected of them but let them know it's okay to make mistakes too. If they are having tests such as an EEG, explain when and how to report symptoms, like telling someone or pushing the button. Reassure them that no symptom is too small or silly. Help take away the pressure of getting it "right."

Support their sensory fears around testing. Be mindful of things like sticky goo, being watched overnight, or needing to bring special food. These little things can cause big stress. Ask what would help and involve them in planning ahead.

Let them ask questions and give real answers. Never assume a child understands just because they're quiet. Give them permission to ask anything, and don't talk over them. Check in often and use words they know.

Be patient during "scrambled brain" moments. If a child is zoning out, stuck, or thinking in a fog, don't push them harder. Help them pause, reset, or step away. Frustration only makes it worse. Let their brain breathe.

Create a safe space to say "I missed that." Angry responses like, "I've already told you that. Didn't you listen?" are not helpful. If a child zones out, let them know it's okay to say so. Be gentle. Don't mock or make them feel silly. Support them with understanding and, when possible, a little humour can help to reduce the pressure.

Watch for signs of zoning out, not just acting out. A blank stare, missed instructions, or strange answers might not be rudeness or inattention. It could be an absence seizure or brain fog. Respond with curiosity, not anger.

Give them ways to laugh, not just cope. When 'scrambled brain' moments pass, it's okay to laugh together. Shared humour is healing. It helps them see they are more than their struggles and still totally lovable.

Remind them: they are enough. The best support isn't always fixing the problem. Sometimes it's just reminding the child, "You are enough, just as you are."

5

Chronic Pain: The Pain You Cannot See

Chronic pain is... exhausting. It's something that's always there, like a shadow that won't go away. Even on the days when it's not too bad, it's still there underneath everything I do, reminding me that I'm never really free from it. Sometimes I wish I could just be asleep or unconscious so I don't have to feel it for a little while. It's hard when no one else can see it. They don't always understand. Just because the pain is invisible, doesn't mean it's not real.

My pain started when I was 12, just before my first period. It is exacerbated around my period as well. The pain is mostly in my ribs. It's not always the same. Sometimes it's a dull ache, and sometimes it's sharp and stabbing. It can come out of nowhere and take my breath away. It's terrifying because I don't know what's going to make it worse or when it's going to flare up. I've been rushed to hospital so many times, doubled up in pain and hardly able to walk. They do all the tests and scans, but they never find anything. "We can't see what's causing it," they say.

That kind of thing messes with your head. You start to wonder, "Is it just me? Am I imagining this?" But I'm not. I have something called nociplastic pain. It's a type of nerve pain that happens when your nervous system doesn't work properly. Mine probably didn't develop properly because I was born really premature. My body sends pain signals, even when there's nothing there to cause pain. It's real, and it hurts.

I've lost count of the number of times I've had to stop doctors or nurses from giving me medications without checking ingredients. I always say, "Can you please check? I'm allergic to dairy." But people roll their eyes or say, "It's just Nurofen" or "It should be fine." One little mistake could kill me. That's not "just fine." One of the worst times was when the pain was so bad I was bent over and could hardly walk. A nurse came with something in a syringe. I asked, "Does it have dairy in it because I'm anaphylactic to dairy?" Her answer? "I don't know. Don't have it then," and she stormed off. I was left there in pain with nothing.

Another time, a person came with pain relief saying it didn't have dairy. They shoved it in my mouth. I asked what it was after having it and they said "just pain relief". I was actually given Endone. They didn't say it was an opioid. They didn't talk about risks or side effects. They just gave it to me like it was nothing. This is how addictions start! It made me feel like I wasn't a person they cared about. I felt like a problem they wanted to shut up. Move her out of emergency to make room for the next patient.

A few days later, they still couldn't find what was wrong. So what did they do? They sent me home with a script for Endone with multiple repeats! No explanation. No talk about how strong it was or what it could do. Just a piece of paper and "off you go." I didn't take it. I didn't want to start down the painkiller addiction path. I just wanted someone to help me. It was so hard to say no to addiction versus something to take the edge off the pain, not make it go away but help a bit. I still sometimes want the Endone but we never fulfilled that script because I didn't want the addiction at twelve years old. It turned out that it was the beginning of period pain and the possibility that I may have endometriosis.

Living with chronic pain isn't just physical. It's mental. It's emotional. It's exhausting. I'm scared to do normal things in case they make it worse. I hesitate before I move the wrong way or carry something too heavy. I stop and ask mydelf, "Is this worth it? Will this land me in hospital again? Will anyone even believe me?"

Eating is hard with my interoception difficulties. People don't always realise, but when my belly feels like it's being stabbed or squeezed tight, the idea of eating can make me feel sick. I *want* to eat, but my body won't let me. Other times, my stomach suddenly feels ready for food and I eat quickly, like I'm starving. It's rare, but it happens, and it might look strange to other people. For me, it's just grabbing that tiny window when eating is actually possible, not painful..

I don't go to hospital anymore when it flares up because I know they can't help me. However, there are some things that do help. Remedial massage helps so much. When someone finally releases those tight trigger points, I feel like I can breathe again. It feels like my body has entered the green zone. It is more helpful than most psychology appointments I have ever had.

There are little comforts too, like soft cushions, weird sleeping positions, or pillows under my back or legs that help me find a comfy spot, even if I look like a twisted pretzel. Heat packs are a lifesaver, especially the stick-on ones I can wear inside my clothes. They are expensive, but they let me keep moving and they are not as heavy as wheat packs.

Sometimes I use YouTube to listen to chronic pain affirmations, healing frequency music, sound baths, or guided meditations. Those things help me calm down and feel like I'm not alone in this. Another thing that helps sounds a bit silly, but it's true. I pretend ChatGPT is my friend. I talk to it and tell it how I feel. It's my own way of processing everything, kind of like the role-playing I did when I was little.

One of the most positive things I've done was join the SKIP program or Supporting Kids in Pain. For a few weeks, I was part of a group of teens who were also living with chronic pain. It was amazing to finally meet other people my age who 'got it'. I didn't have to explain everything. They just knew. I gave each of them one of my soft, silent sensory fidgets—a Cozipal or a Sensorian—to help them cope. I found out later that one girl's occupational therapist used her Cozipal to help her body understand that safe touch was possible again. It helped her heal from Complex Regional Pain Syndrome. Knowing that something I created made a difference in her healing—that was incredible!

Homeschooling also helps. On bad nights when I can't sleep from the pain, I don't have to rush out the door the next morning like kids in regular school. I can rest if I need to. That makes a huge difference when brushing your teeth or doing your hair feels like you're being stabbed. Everything takes longer. Please realise, I'm not lazy. I'm in pain.

I carry this pain with me every single day, and I keep going. I keep speaking up, even when it's hard. I keep helping others when I can. I keep showing up for myself. Even though the pain can't be seen—it's always there. The only funny thing about the pain? I once tried to use my guinea pigs as heat packs over the sore part, but they refused to lie on the painful spot! What they *do* love doing is lying on me just enough to reach over and scrape their claws across my very sensitive belly button.

Not helpful, piggies! Not helpful!

Chronic pain is real, even if the tests come back normal. Just because doctors can't find anything on a scan or a blood test doesn't mean we're making it up. Even if you can't see it, believe us when we say something hurts.

Take time to listen to us. Don't rush in with a prescription and then leave. Ask us what we've tried already, what makes it worse, and what gives even a tiny bit of relief. Having someone who listens helps more than you realise.

Always check for allergies before giving medication. Never assume something is safe. Each brand of drug may contain different ingredients. One small mistake could be life-threatening, so double-check every ingredient, every time.

Don't pressure us to push through pain. Pain changes everything. It can slow us down when we're getting dressed, trying to concentrate, brushing our teeth, or just getting out of bed. Telling us to "get on with it" only makes it harder.

Help us find what works, which may not be medicine. Sometimes it's a heat pack, a soft blanket, a warm bath, or a gentle massage. Sometimes it's rest or just lying in a comfy position watching television. Support us in trying things that soothe our bodies.

Give us flexibility when we're in pain. Pain can wreck our sleep or leave us drained the next day. Let us move at our own pace and rest when we need to.

Understand how we eat. If we're suddenly eating more, we might finally be feeling okay enough to eat. If we're avoiding food, it could be because we're feeling nauseous or our stomach hurts. Respect that our appetite is sometimes linked to our pain.

Support programs like SKIP that bring kids with pain together are great. Being around people who "get it" can change everything. These programs can make us feel less alone and give us tools to manage things better. (If your child feels alone, they could always email Our Pixie Friends in Sprizzletania and the pixies will respond.)

Let us help others too. Just because we're hurting doesn't mean we have nothing to give. Helping others, especially kids going through similar experiences, can help us feel strong again. We can feel empowered to make a difference through shared experiences.

Kindness and patience go a long way. Being calm, gentle, and fully present can sometimes help more than anything else. When you treat us with kindness, it eases our nervous systems. That can be powerful pain relief.

6

Bowel/Bladder Dysfunction: Body Embarrassment

There's something I don't talk about much, and that's because for a long time, it made me feel really embarrassed. I felt like I wasn't 'normal'. Like something was 'wrong' with me, and that I should hide it. The truth is, I have bowel and bladder dysfunction. It's something most people don't see, but it has affected so many parts of my life in ways that are hard to explain.

Because of my bladder issues, I had to wear nappies much longer than other kids. I didn't just wear them as a baby. I needed them during my early school years too. I had to wear nappies on school excursions, on the school bus, at sleepovers, birthday parties, and pretty much any time we left home. That included trips in the car or even short walks. I always had to be prepared, just in case I couldn't hold on. It became a part of my routine, but not one that made me proud.

Being different made me a target. Kids can be cruel, especially when they notice something that stands out. I was teased a lot for wearing nappies. People would say things like, "Only babies wear nappies," which is often said to help toddlers learn to use the toilet. When you're older and have a real medical condition, those words don't help. They hurt. It felt like those comments got stuck in my head and started to define how I saw myself: as gross, as babyish, as not normal. After a while, I even started to believe them.

I wanted so badly to be like the other kids. I thought if I just stopped wearing nappies, I'd be okay. I tried hard to give them up, even though my body clearly wasn't ready. I kept wetting the bed, no matter how much I hoped I wouldn't. Sometimes, I honestly thought I was dry. I'd say to Mum, "My nappy is dry!" because I couldn't feel that it was wet. My nerves didn't work properly, so I didn't get the signals that other kids did.

Carrying that shame around felt like dragging a heavy backpack that no one else could see. I felt excluded from normal childhood activities, and I didn't even have the words to explain why. I just knew that my body didn't work like everyone else's, and I didn't understand why. That's actually why I came up with *Our Pixie Friends* when I was six years old. I didn't want other kids to feel the way I did—alone, broken, ashamed. I wanted them to know they are not the only ones.

One day that sticks in my mind was when I was about six or seven and we were at the shops. Mum bought me a small apple juice. After I drank it, I needed to go to the toilet right away. Then it happened again ... and again. I went to the toilet about seven times in a row. In the end, Mum had to take me home (with a nappy on in the car) because I couldn't manage to go more than a few minutes without needing to go again. Later, the doctor told us that my bladder could only hold 15 to 20 millilitres.

Being told my bladder worked like a toddler's even though I was six, and that I might have a bladder the size of a 6-year-old's by the time I was about 13, was crushing. It made me feel even more broken. I was trying so hard to do what other kids could do without thinking about it, and it still wasn't enough. At school, it was hard to focus because I often needed to go to the bathroom. That meant I would miss the next part of the lesson.

We ended up going to the Mars Clinic for help. That's where the physiotherapists attached wires to my private parts to see how my muscles were working. I had to sit on a special computer toilet while they measured how my bladder and pelvic floor muscles were behaving. It was really awkward and uncomfortable. They tried to help me learn control through a game where I had to make a fairy or dolphin jump on a screen by squeezing the right muscles. It looked fun, but I didn't understand what I was doing to make the fairy move. After a few sessions, they told Mum it wasn't working because I had very little control. I did like the fairy, even if I didn't know how to make her fly.

Because of my neurodiversity, I didn't always know who it was okay to talk to about my medical needs. I once told a group of Year 3 boys about my having to wear nappies. I thought I was just being honest, but they laughed and teased me. I wish someone had helped me understand who I could safely talk to and who might not understand.

The fear of kids finding out stayed with me for a long time. Kids can be brutal when they don't understand something. When they think you're different in a "babyish" way, they don't always stop to think about what's really going on. Even though I knew deep down it wasn't my fault, I still felt like I was letting everyone down, like I should be doing better. Those fears still come up sometimes. Even now, I get scared I won't be able to hold on, or that someone will find out and laugh. But I've also learned to be kinder to myself. I try to remind myself that my body isn't bad. It's just different, and different doesn't mean broken. It just means I've had to find different kinds of strength.

One wonderful mother of a friend invited me to my first sleepover. She kindly sat all the girls down and we talked about my needing to wear a nappy. It made it okay. It brought it out into the open so I had nothing to hide, nothing to be ashamed about. It gave the kids a chance to develop tolerance because they could ask questions and learn in a safe space. In my experience, whenever adults are more open and honest about medical issues, it gives everyone a chance to learn. It creates space for kindness and understanding instead of shame and judgement when kids ask questions in public.

Even now, the bladder issues haven't fully gone away. I still sometimes need to wear a nappy at night, especially if I've had something to drink with my tablets before bed. I lie awake wondering if I'm going to wet the bed, or wake up cold and soaked. That fear repeats in my head and makes it really hard to fall asleep. It's exhausting mentally and physically.

Going to the toilet can be painful too. Chronic constipation is another aspect of my bowel and bladder dysfunction. I had to have Osmolax for more than 10 years, and sometimes it wasn't enough. It's not always just about needing to go. Sometimes it hurts. Sometimes I need distractions to help me cope—like a toy, a story, or just something to focus on that isn't the pain. Little things like that make a huge difference. When I was young, Mum would read me books or play hand clapping games sometimes to distract me from the pain or while we were waiting for my body to work.

There were nights when I lay silently under the blankets because I didn't want to wake Mum. She never got mad at me for being wet or when she had to wash all the sheets, blankets and quilts, but I didn't want to be a burden. I didn't want to make her tired or upset, so I just lay there, cold and wet, wishing I could be like the other kids. Wishing I could be 'normal'. I already had so many other medical things going on—heart issues, scrambled brain episodes, asthma, eczema, allergies, anaphylaxis and sensory processing difficulties. The bladder problems just felt like another reminder that my body didn't work the way it was supposed to.

What makes it worse is that people don't talk about things like this. Not in schools. Not in books. Not in families. Definitely not in front of friends. There's this huge silence around bowel and bladder problems, like it's something to be hidden. But when we don't talk about it, it just adds more shame. So this is my truth and I'm sharing it because I know there are other kids out there going through the same thing. Kids who are scared, ashamed, or tired of feeling like their body is wrong. If that's you, please know this: you're not alone.

Key Takeaways:

Teach children that everybody is different. Read books and listen to positive messages in stories and music about how each person is unique and precious. Build the child's own self-esteem, but also encourage kindness and acceptance of everybody.

Be honest and open about why some kids need nappies. If adults explain things clearly and without shame, other kids are more likely to understand instead of tease. Openness helps build empathy and stops bullying before it starts. When we tell the truth, when we're real and honest, that's when the shame starts to shrink. That's when things begin to feel lighter.

Never say things like "only babies wear nappies" when encouraging toilet training. Comments like that stick in children's minds and can easily be repeated to others which can be hurtful. Choose words that support, not shame.

Make it totally okay to wear nappies. Let kids know it doesn't make them "less". In fact, having extra needs doesn't make them weaker. It can mean they're strong in other ways. Let them feel special and valued, not embarrassed or humiliated.

Know that bowel or bladder dysfunction can be a real medical issue. It's not always something a child can just grow out of, like regular bed-wetting. Some kids take years to improve. Be patient and never blame them. It's not something they're doing wrong.

Teach neurodivergent kids who it's safe to tell. They might not automatically know which adults or kids they can trust with private things. Help them understand who is safe to talk to, but never make them feel ashamed for needing support.

Support children who cannot feel if they are wet or dry. Some children genuinely can't feel wetness or leaks due to sensory issues or medical conditions. Confusion can be disguised as anger or denial.

Include the child in conversations about their care. Don't talk over them or act like they're invisible. Speak with them, not about them. It helps them feel respected and in control of their own body.

Use gentle distractions during toilet time if needed. For some kids, using the toilet can feel scary or painful. Books, calming music, toys, or gentle stories can help make it feel safer and less stressful.

Show acceptance through your words and actions. When adults are kind, open, and supportive, kids feel seen and safe. That's where confidence starts—with being accepted exactly as you are.

7

The Magic of Appointments

Hospital appointments have always been a regular part of my life, from the time I left the special care nursery right through to today. Different hospitals, different doctors, different reasons, different tests and treatments. It's just been part of how things are for me. Sometimes it's been regular, others it's been unexpected, but it's always been there.

For a while in Year 1, I had appointments every Thursday after I detipped my finger. It went on for about three months, and for that short time, Thursdays became my hospital days. No school, just going to the hospital. After that period ended, hospital days didn't stop. I have had many trips to emergency and scheduled specialist appointments throughout my childhood. When you see an allergist, dermatologist, endocrinologist, gastroenterologist, paediatrician, urologist, neurologist ... the appointments add up.

Lots of people assume that if you go to hospital often, you must be staying overnight on a ward with a comfy bed and television to entertain you, but that is not true for all of us. I've only had that experience a few times. I've had many full days at hospital for just a single outpatient appointment. It is about a three-hour round trip in the car; longer during peak hour. If I had a morning appointment at 8.15am, we had to leave home around 6.15, which meant getting up even earlier. Then came the waiting.

I usually had to wait for hours in the waiting room. At one of the clinics, they gave all the kids the same appointment time, so we were all sitting around for ages with nothing to do. Things did improve after COVID. These days, waiting rooms are no longer filled with patients waiting for hours and hours. That has been a big improvement. It has made the whole experience in hospital feel less overwhelming.

I have had countless trips to emergency. That meant even more time in waiting rooms, then hours in emergency cubicles, sitting there while nurses and doctors went back and forth, waiting on test results and treatment decisions. Emergency visits were long and tiring and often filled with fear, pain and uncertainty. Because I arrived in emergency very late one night, the kids' ward had closed and I was moved to the adult emergency ward, opposite a man who was very drunk, violent and abusive. Mum closed my curtain, but I clung to her, absolutely petrified. Luckily, a kind nurse came and realised I was fearful, so she found another cubicle around the corner for me. I was very grateful.

One time I waited three hours for a clinic appointment, but something really great happened. The hospital volunteers came by with a trolley full of activities and games to choose from. They were so kind and fun. It broke the boredom. That moment stuck with me. It's part of why I created *Our Pixie Friends*. I wanted kids who were feeling unwell, anxious, or stuck waiting in hospitals to have something to entertain them. On our website, kids can listen to audio stories even if they don't feel up to reading or doing anything too draining.

Some of the most important parts of hospital days didn't happen inside the hospital. They happened in the car. The car became a little bubble just for Mum and me. On the way there, we'd talk, or sometimes not talk. Sometimes I'd stare out the window, especially if I was nervous. Mum never forced me to chat. She just let me be. She might play music, hold my hand (when I was heavy enough to sit in the front seat), or tell a funny story to distract me. We would play imaginative games like pretending to be police chasing the car in front of us, or making up creative songs or stories. After the appointment, the car was where I could cry, celebrate, or just be quiet. There was one day I remember clearly. I was too scared to speak. I just stared out the window trying to keep it all together. Mum didn't try to make me talk. She just gently held my hand. That silence said everything. I wasn't alone. That's the kind of mum she is—not just physically there, but there with love.

She didn't just take me to appointments. She got me through them. She would pack books or colouring or install fun apps on her phone. She would always pack my favourite safe food for after my appointments. If I was tired, she'd stroke my hair while I lay on her lap. If I was scared, we prayed together, or she told stories or sang along with my CD's to keep me calm. As I got older, and the appointments became more frequent, she still made it special in new ways. A drive-thru treat. A new app. A big cuddle. A whispered, "You did so well today, sweetheart." She never stopped showing up, even when she was tired. Even when I felt like I was too much to handle, she always found a way to tell me I was worth it, to let me know I was valued.

After the long car ride, the waiting room and the appointment, it helped to have something fun to look forward to. Mum tried to make sure of that. One of my fondest memories is the jelly. I know it sounds silly, but it meant a lot. After fasting, or a blood test, or just being brave, I'd get a cup of jelly from the café. It came in a container with a tiny spoon. Red was my favourite, but sometimes I got green or orange, and that jelly wasn't just a treat. It was the *one and only* safe food I could have from the café. That made it even more special. It was comfort. It told me I had done well, that I was strong, that I was still a kid, even in the middle of a serious day. When they renovated the café and stopped having the jelly, I was really disappointed. Now there is nothing safe for me to eat there at all—only bottled drinks. It's just not the same.

Other things I loved were the piano that anyone was allowed to play and the hospital playground. The Queensland Children's Hospital has an absolutely magical one. I'm really glad they opened it while I was still little, because the old hospital didn't have fun places like that. The playground had a huge hollow tree with giant ants and bees you could climb on. I also loved the giant crocodile statues. I loved climbing on the big dome. Every time we visited, I could get a little higher. I felt so proud when I finally reached the top. Mum clapped and cheered every time I progressed.

Then there was the Starlight Room. It's a space inside the hospital, but it feels like something from a whole different world with colourful walls, music, crafts, games and Captain Starlight being funny and wild. It didn't smell like hospital or feel serious. It felt like fun. It helped me forget what I had just been through. It gave me relief, a sense of safety.

One of my favourite things in the Starlight Room was the huge TV with *Just Dance* on it. I would dance for ages, even if I was sore. I just needed to move. In a place where everything is controlled—your meds, your tests, your food—dancing gave me a little bit of freedom. I got to pick the song. I got to decide how I danced. I got to laugh if I wanted. And then there was the flip table. When it lay horizontally, you could play games like air hockey, but it could rotate and when it was vertical you could play different games. It was amazing!

You never knew what was inside the Starlight Room that day, and that made it exciting. If I was nervous or tired of being asked questions, I could play. I could control what I did, what I played with, what my body did. Captain Starlight would play Mario Cart with me, and Mum would too. We didn't need to talk. There was shared understanding that Captain Starlight cared about me and wasn't going to poke me with needles. That room was our little calm spot; an island of peace in the middle of a medical storm. I also got to meet some other kids from the hospital and it helped me feel less alone. I wasn't just a patient. I was a 'normal' kid having fun.

These appointments were exhausting and often scary. I never knew what to expect. Was there going to be another scary test, a blood test, an x-ray or something unknown? Emergency visits could be long and overwhelming, but in the middle of all the hard stuff, there were also moments of magic. Being given a sticker or a cuddle, eating jelly, climbing a tree, dancing or playing a game really helped.

Key Takeaways:

Plan for long days. If a child has a hospital or emergency appointment, help them prepare by talking through the schedule, bringing comfort items, and packing snacks, water, and quiet activities.

Create positive routines. Little rituals like a special food, a quiet drive, a favourite song, or a "you did well" cuddle after the appointment can make a hard day feel safer.

Be aware of food safety needs. If a child has allergies or medical dietary needs, bring safe food with you to avoid disappointment, hunger and distress. You never know how long you will be there. (Mum used to keep a stash of baby food in pouches in the boot of the car for emergency trips to hospital because I could never eat the hospital food.)

Offer comfort without pressure. Some kids don't want to talk about how they feel before, during or after appointments. Just sitting beside them, holding their hand, or letting them stare out the window can be enough. Let them process what's happening in a calm, supportive environment. If they want to talk, be fully present and really listen to them. Mum would look at me, not her phone. I was important to her.

Give kids something to look forward to. Whether it's a playground visit, listening to a story, colouring, or dancing, build in small moments of joy before or after medical appointments or scary procedures.

Empower kids with choices. Let them choose the playlist, pick a sticker, decide what to play with, or how to move. Even small decisions help them feel more in control.

Don't underestimate the impact of play. Giving children the chance to climb, create, move, or imagine, even in a hospital, isn't just fun. It is helping them to heal.

Acknowledge bravery. Even if they cried, tell them they were brave. Your words help shape how they see themselves.

Focus on who they are, not just what they're going through. Remind them that they are a special child, not just a patient. They deserve kindness, fun, rest, and space to just be themselves.

Mental Health

8

Anxiety: The Fear of 'What If?'

Anxiety has been a part of me for as long as I can remember. It started before I even had the words to explain the feelings. I was born early (3 months too early) and had to be resuscitated three or four times a day. My brain's alarm system, the amygdala, was always firing, letting me know I was about to die because I couldn't breathe. It was always on, always alert. Mum could not hold me and tell me it was going to be okay. If she was holding me when the alarms went off and I needed to be resuscitated, the nurses would snatch me off her and place me right back into the humidicrib so I could be 'bagged' and my little heart could be pumped. My fight or flight response was constantly in overdrive. There was no comfort, just alarms, fear and panic. Those early experiences shaped how my brain developed. My body decided it was never safe.

The fears continued as I grew. As a toddler, I was absolutely petrified of the nebuliser mask - the sound, the smell and the feeling on my face. It was like the anaesthetic mask they used when I had my hernia surgery at 6 months. I also had a deep fear of lying down at night because I thought I'd vomit, and vomit I did, often a few times a day for 5-10 minutes at a time, severely decreasing my weight, until they diagnosed my dairy allergy. They tried soy formula, formula for babies with allergies and formula for the babies who were allergic to the formula for babies with allergies. I had multiple doctors' appointments, blood tests, scary needle prick allergy tests which all contributed to ... a phobia of doctors.

This was also the time when we lost our house due to a family breakup. Mum and I were homeless and going between my sister's place and my Grandparents' house. We were so lucky and we are so grateful to have had such loving, caring family during that time, but it was also stressful. I never knew where I was going to be, and where was Daddy? Where was my house? Why was Mummy smiling when I could feel her brain was sad? Why was my little nephew pulling my hair? (He was only one and didn't understand that it hurt.) Why was my sister angry that I had thrown up on her new rug? I'm sorry. I'm sorry. I'm sorry.

I reached the point when I was at family day care, that I just chanted, "Mummy, Mummy, Mummy" all day. The poor day care lady tried everything, but nothing worked to calm me. My neonatologist referred me to Dr Elisabeth Hoehn, the most amazing child psychiatrist (who helped me for the next 10-11 years). By the time I was two, I had already been diagnosed with Generalised Anxiety Disorder. She said I needed stability. Things had to change so Mum took three months off work just to be with me and we moved into my Grandparents' house where Grandpa became my father figure. Grandma, Grandpa and Mum spent so much time snuggling me. Their cuddles and deep pressure helped me feel calm again. I needed Mum close to know I wouldn't be left alone, to know I was safe.

By the time I was six, I had PTSD. It happened after I found my Grandma unconscious on the floor, lying in a pool of blood. After that, every time I went out, I would need to check if she was okay. We would often have to ring home just so I could hear her voice to know she was okay. As soon as we arrived back home, I would run to her and check her head to see that the scar was still there, that she wasn't bleeding. It took almost 12 months before I gradually stopped doing this.

I was scared of everything, and I mean everything. I was afraid of parties, people, dogs, food, loud noises, crowds and big kids. I had food anxiety after three episodes of anaphylaxis when I was 4. I started panicking about what I ate. I was terrified I would die. New places made me freeze. I didn't want to go. I couldn't trust what might happen. What if I got sick? What if there was something I couldn't eat? What if something went wrong and no one was there to help me?

Even when I knew something was "probably okay," my body didn't believe it. People would say, "just calm down," or "take a deep breath," but it didn't help. When your nervous system is completely on fire, words like that feel useless. It made me feel like it was my fault, like I was doing something wrong, but I wasn't. My brain was literally wired for fear.

My emetophobia (fear of vomiting) increased when I was about 8, after I had been on school camp and a boy had thrown up on me, resulting in my coming out in hives then missing out on the rest of the fun activities, but it really took hold after my nephew had a sleepover and was sick in the doorway to my room. I went into full-blown panic. I was trapped inside the room until Mum cleaned it up. The sight and smell were truly overwhelming. I couldn't settle. Mum had to take my nephew home because I wasn't coping. He was fine. He felt much better, but I was a mess. I couldn't stop panicking. When she got home, Mum had to cuddle me for over 40 minutes before I could calm down enough to get to sleep - that reassuring deep pressure that calmed me when I was younger. That fear stays with me even today, but becoming a sports trainer has helped. I can deal with it a bit better now, as long as it is someone else being sick and not me. Constant nausea and the fear of anaphylaxis don't help.

Starting any new medication is a massive stress for me. I can't trust that what's written on the box tells the whole story. Often, doctors and pharmacists don't even know all the ingredients. Lactose is a particular worry for me. One allergist told us the lactose in tablets was safe, that it was derived from milk sugars not milk proteins, but when I contacted the manufacturer of one medication, they replied that their lactose was *derived from dairy* and *not suitable* for people with a dairy allergy. So why is there no allergen warning label on the box like there is with food? Why do pharmacists not have access to this information to keep their patients safe?

When I was little, Mum was putting zinc cream on my skin, until they suddenly started adding peanut oil to it. She had no idea until she investigated why it was causing a rash and she checked the new ingredients. If I had gotten it on my hands and put my hands in my mouth, that could have killed me. Chemists often change the brand of a drug they stock, which means I have to start the whole investigation again from scratch—calling manufacturers or hunting around for a chemist that has the brand I already know is safe. Why do different brands have different fillers and colours that can cause a reaction? It's exhausting.

One of the scariest times was before a new medical treatment. I'd been prescribed a medication called Dupixent for my eczema. I had read every possible side effect and had worked myself into a full-blown panic. That night, I wrote myself this letter:

Raw, Real, and Vulnerable – A Note the Night Before Treatment

10:14pm, Sunday 29th June 2025

It feels kind of weird to write this, but as I'm writing an autobiography, why not be real, raw and vulnerable, right?
So tomorrow is a big day. I might be having my treatment ... might not. Every single thing I read contradicts the other... I don't know what to do. I know the doctors will just encourage me to do this treatment because that's all they know.
We don't know the long-term effects. We just read that there are correlations to cancer ... and joint pain ... people drop in the middle of the street with a knee that just gives out ... you could die from anaphylaxis ... it could cause anything. And the bad thing about it is that we don't know 'til we try it. We don't know how my body will respond ... if it will behave. If it doesn't ... then this might be my last night.
My last wake-up at 6am ... my last gym session ... my last meal ... last dessert ... my last day ... I don't even have that. Maybe I should've lived a little ... done more in life. Let myself live. I'm just in a constant state of worry and I value every breath I breathe right now ... because I might stop breathing tomorrow. My heart might stop beating. What if? What if?
I'm tingling with nerves. I write this to tell you how we really feel. So

please, when I walk into your office, answer every single question I have, because what if?
Going through all the text messages of things that I've said yes to, but now I'm wondering ... will I actually get to go there? See that place? Go to that party? Live my life? Have another birthday? Do that speech ... plan that talk? Write that book?
I often imagine what it would be like for my Mum if I had died from anaphylaxis ... in the NICU ... during convulsions, etc. The text messages ... the calls ... what would she say? What if I die tomorrow? What commitments will she have to tell people no to?
I might have less than 24 hours. I might have more. If I have more time, I'd live. I'd do all the things I don't feel like doing because what if it could be the last? I wonder what the last thing I'd ever do is. I wonder if it's saying to someone I feel funny after having the treatment ... the injection ... or struggling to breathe. I just hope that if it were to happen ... it'd be quick. I hope I don't have to get resuscitated. I really want to live.
– Siobhan Wilson, 16

For me, anxiety is like having hundreds of little boxes in my brain. Each box holds a worry or a memory or a fear. When one thing upsets me, it's like a key opens that box, then another one, then another, like dominoes falling. Suddenly, it's an avalanche. All the boxes are opening, and all the feelings come rushing out at once. Once, my psychiatrist asked me to create a "worry box." Mum took me shopping and let me pick a special box to use. That night before bed, I had to write down my worries so I could "put them away" in the box and sleep. Well, that didn't work! As soon as I started with one worry, all the others began pouring out. All the little boxes of trauma in my brain started popping open. After 30 minutes and 40 worries on sticky notes, Mum finally said,

"That's enough." She gently stopped me. But I couldn't stop myself. It was like the worry had unlocked something deeper.

There was another time at a mobile farm experience. Everyone else was having fun, getting close to the baby animals. I wasn't. I saw the animals and my body just reacted. I completely panicked and ran—straight up my sister's partner. I didn't even think. I climbed him like a goanna up a tree and perched on his shoulders, desperate to get away, to be safe. It was like my body had one goal: get as far away and as high up as possible. I felt ridiculous afterward, but in the moment, it felt like the only safe option. That's the thing with anxiety—it doesn't wait for logic. It just takes over.

Another huge anxiety trigger for me was dogs. I was absolutely petrified of them. I remember one time a dog was on a leash but ran in circles around me and tangled me up in the lead. I froze. I was completely stuck and couldn't move. My heart pounded like crazy. I didn't care that the dog wasn't "dangerous". It felt unpredictable, and that made it terrifying. Looking back, I think that fear came from something deeper. When I was living at my sister's house, she had a dog. It had sharp claws and it was unpredictable. When it ran over the top of me, it hurt and scared me. I was already in survival mode, not feeling safe, so every bark, every jump, every little sound or movement sent me into a state of panic. The fear wasn't just about the dog. It was about not being safe.

But it hasn't all been bad. My brother had a dog when I was a bit older, and he did something that helped. He saw I was scared and didn't laugh at me or tell me to 'get over it'. He stood between me and the dog while he patted it to show me it was gentle. Then he had the dog lie down at one end of the hallway and he sat down between me and the dog, continually patting it. I gradually came closer with Mum holding my hand. Then, gently, he encouraged me to pat the dog. The next day, I was right next to that dog, patting it by myself. He made me feel safe. I was so proud of myself for overcoming that challenge. I was scared, but I did it. That moment gave me hope. These days, I'm better. I don't have to cross the street just because there's a dog half a kilometre away. I don't freeze like I used to. I can handle it.

At different stages of my life, I've tried lots of different relaxation strategies to help me cope. For a while, I had a little soft toy called *Worry Bunny*. Each night, I was allowed to tell it just one worry before bed, and it would do the worrying for me while I slept. That helped for a while. We also had a balloon pump decorated with fairy stickers. Mum turned it into a "magic fairy dust puffer." At bedtime, I would lie down, close my eyes, and she would puff the "fairy dust" along my arms and legs. That helped my body feel calm and safe. I loved anything to do with magic and fairies. We even had a fairy ring in our back yard. I think it helped me feel less alone. I would sometimes write my worries down and send those letters to the fairies. When I was six, I wrote my first book, *Sakaela the Sneezy Pixie Visits Amy*. In it, the pixie uses Magic Pixie Crystals to help the little girl feel brave. I then developed those Magic Pixie Crystals which I also used myself. They helped me feel brave too. I've always loved using magic to help myself feel calm.

Other things helped too: meditations, relaxation music, handpan music, white noise, soft, silent sensory fidgets and going to peaceful, quiet spaces where I could close off from the world. I even had a little tent over my bed that I filled with cuddly toys to make it feel like my own safe cave. I used essential oils too, because for me, all the senses help.

I've learned that patient adults are safe adults. I've learned that different strategies can help me at different times, and that I can heal from the things that have happened in my life.

Key Takeaways:

Don't say, "Just relax" because it doesn't help. When anxiety takes over, it can feel like our whole body is stressed and tense. We can't always talk about it, but we can feel it—tight chests, sore tummies, frozen limbs. Saying "just relax" makes us feel like you don't understand. Hold us gently (or using deep pressure if we're okay with that) and stay calm so we can feel your kindness. Help us feel safe in our bodies first. Then the thoughts will follow.

Understand that anxiety can come from early trauma. Some of us have had scary things happen even as babies. That fear can stay in our bodies and brains and affect how we react later on, even if we don't remember it. What seems like a small thing to you, may be a trigger for us.

Some kids need to be near someone safe just to survive. Needing to be close may not be 'clinginess' or bad behaviour. Understand our need for reassurance to feel safe enough to explore the world. Feeling close to a safe adult can help our nervous system calm down and stop us from panicking. https://www.circleofsecuritynetwork.org/the_circle_of_security.html

Answer every question with patience, even the tenth time. We're not trying to annoy you. Repeating questions is often about needing reassurance. We need your steady voice to feel safe again.

Don't rush us into scary things. Trying new foods or patting animals might feel terrifying to some kids. Stay close, go slowly, and guide us gently. We need to know you're there to protect us.

Predictability helps calm our brains. Surprises can feel scary to an anxious child. Let us know what's coming, give us time to prepare, and try not to change plans suddenly.

Try different sensory tools to find what works. Some kids like hard, crunchy things. Others need soft, silent ones. There is no one-size-fits-all. Let us experiment and respect our preferences.

Let us bring someone we trust to hard things. Medical appointments, scary events, or big changes are easier to face with a trusted adult beside us. Don't make us go alone if we're not ready. If we have been stressed and need to leave, that's okay too. I had to go home after a special event in Kindy because I didn't cope with the crowd and changes in routine.

Give us space to be honest about our fears. Let us say "I'm scared" without being shut down, dismissed or laughed at. Believing us builds trust. That trust helps us feel less alone.

Sometimes silence and presence are more powerful than words. Just standing nearby, sitting close, or holding our hand can calm us more than any big speech. You don't have to fix everything. Being there can help.

Playful rituals and magical thinking can help. Things like fairy dust, worry bunnies, Cozipals or Magic Pixie Crystals can be very helpful. The imagination is a powerful thing, as are positive thoughts. Imagination gives us hope and courage in ways that make sense to us.

Learn what anxiety looks like in the body. It's not always words. Watch for signs like wide pupils, pale skin, frozen faces, shaky hands, or quick breathing. Complaining that our finger hurts or we have a headache are all signs we're not okay.

Remember: what you see is just the tip of the iceberg. We might seem calm or "fine" on the outside, but inside we could be drowning. Most of what we're going through is hidden. Please look deeper.

9

PTSD and OCD: Living in Survival Mode

Most people don't see fear when they look at a plate, a fork, a pen, or take a breath of air—but I do. I didn't always. I used to just eat, breathe, hold a pen, and come home without overthinking any of it. I used to feel safe. But now, everything feels like a possible danger. That's what PTSD has done to me. Trauma isn't just about bad memories, flashbacks, nightmares and physical body reactions. It's about constantly being on edge. It's about the tiny things no one sees—things you can't explain without people thinking you're overreacting. To me, it's not silly. It's not dramatic. It's not obsessive. It's survival.

I was only six. I didn't know what trauma was. I didn't know what Post Traumatic Stress Disorder (PTSD) meant. I just knew something really scary had happened. I walked in and saw my Grandma unconscious on the floor, in a pool of blood. She was in and out of consciousness and all she said was to go get Mummy. She had food poisoning, but I didn't know that at the time. I didn't even know food poisoning could do that. What I saw was her body, not moving, blood around her. No words. No reassurance. No safety. Just silence and stillness and something that felt really, really wrong.

My heart stopped. I froze. Then I ran to Mum. She was busy ringing the ambulance and getting Grandpa up. I was all alone. I cried. I couldn't stop thinking about it. Even though she recovered, the fear didn't leave. From that day on, I had to call her every time we left the house. I needed to hear her voice. I needed to know she was still alive. If she didn't answer straight away, I felt physically sick. My stomach would drop. My hands would shake. I couldn't concentrate. Even when Mum said she was probably in the bathroom or would call back soon, my brain didn't believe it. It said, "No. Something's happened. Go home. Check. Fix it."

Coming home wasn't easy either. As soon as the car pulled in, I jumped out and ran through the front door. I just had to find Grandma, to see if she was breathing, talking, moving. I had to see her face. I had to see the scar on her head to make sure it wasn't bleeding. I had to know she was okay. I did that every single time for almost twelve months. It wasn't a phase. It wasn't a choice. It wasn't something I could stop. My body wouldn't let me even after she'd been fine for months and people told me, "She's fine now. You don't need to worry." Even after she laughed and told me not to stress, I still had to check. It wasn't about logic. It was about what my brain had learned—that safety could be taken away without warning. People can look fine and suddenly collapse. The people you love most can disappear in a second. Blood, stillness and silence could be waiting behind any door.

Even now, ten years later, I panic when someone doesn't answer the phone, takes too long in the bathroom, or lies too still. I picture blood. I freeze, then check. That's what trauma does. It teaches your body to live on high alert. That's how obsessive compulsive behaviours can grow out of trauma. Your brain is trying to keep you safe because it doesn't want to let it happen again, so it makes rules, compulsions and routines to protect you. Soon, it feels like if you don't do those things, something bad will happen. Not might ... will.

When I had refractory anaphylaxis, everything got worse. I already lived with food allergies. I already knew what anaphylaxis was, but that night was different. My body didn't respond to adrenaline. I needed dose after dose. I thought I was going to die. I didn't just think it; I asked aloud, over and over, "Am I going to die?" because it really felt like I might. After that, nothing felt safe anymore, especially not food. Even if someone promised it was safe, even if the label said "dairy free," even if they were trained staff, I still didn't believe them. My brain said, "They're wrong. They forgot something. They don't understand. They made a mistake. They don't care enough." And sometimes, people did get it wrong. Sometimes people did roll their eyes. That just confirmed my fears that other people could not be trusted.

That's when the routines started. Mum had to buy me my own toaster, my own jug, my own plastic plates, bowls, and cutlery; not because she thought it was necessary, but because I couldn't eat otherwise. Even at home, I couldn't use the regular forks. I didn't want to drink from a glass unless I knew it hadn't touched anything dairy-related. I started cutting steak with a plastic knife, not because it worked well (it didn't), but because my brain said, "What if the metal touched something dangerous? What if you don't wipe it and its your last regret?"

I wiped every plate and piece of cutlery before I used them. It didn't matter if I watched them come straight from the dishwasher, if they were clean. I washed my hands before eating—not just when they were dirty, but because I might have touched something unsafe. What if someone sneezed near my food? What if a crumb stuck to my hand and I didn't notice?

Even pens started to feel dangerous. What if someone used one right after eating something risky? What if allergens were on the surface? I couldn't take the risk. I avoided writing and then eating. Even my own laptop started to feel unsafe. What if I touched it after being exposed to something? I avoided touching other people's computers completely.

It didn't stop there. I started worrying about breathing in cars, buildings, and unfamiliar rooms. What if someone ate nuts earlier? What if the particles are in the air vents? What if I breathe them in? That's how far it goes. Even essential oils weren't safe. I worried about how they were made—was dairy involved in production? Medication didn't feel safe. I contacted manufacturers to confirm ingredients, even for things I'd taken before. My brain doesn't care about "probably." It only responds to "what if?" Mashed potato became a trigger for me. That was what I'd eaten the night of my worst reaction. The one I was told was safe. Now, when I see it, I feel sick. I can't explain the fear in words. My body and brain still remember that it was mashed potato that nearly killed me.

People don't see any of this. They just see me wiping a spoon, using my clothes to 'wipe off' allergens, refusing food, or asking a lot of questions. They assume I'm fussy or dramatic, but the compulsions don't make me feel better. They stop me from feeling completely out of control. Logically, I know the spoon is probably clean. I know the pen probably doesn't have anything on it. I know the food might be safe, but the trauma part of my brain reacts before I can finish the thought, "It's fine."

I don't do sleepovers. I don't eat out or buy takeaways. I pack my own food to take to family and business events. I check every new product over and over, checking not only packaging labels but also manufacturer websites. I avoid touching public objects. I plan exits. I scan rooms. I plan where paramedics can gain access if needed. I make excuses to move away from people eating. I worry if they've eaten something or drunk coffee with milk that I will have anaphylaxis if they breathe on me, so I lean back or step back. Then I worry they'll think I'm being rude.

Surviving isn't the same as living. Surviving means constantly scanning, preparing, bracing. When people say, "You'll be fine," or "Just trust me," they don't understand. I'm not trying to be fussy. I'm trying to stay alive. I don't trust easily because I've learned that even well-meaning people can get it wrong. Trusting too quickly can hurt me, or worse. I wish adults could see that. I wish they knew that when I ask about food, or avoid a room, or skip a meal, it's not about them. It's that I don't trust any more. I've seen what happens when "safe" isn't.

When I met Bill Blaikie, author of *Back From the Brink - PTSD: The Human Cost of Military Service*, Mum asked him what helped him recover from his PTSD. He explained that it was learning to let the past go and realising he is safe now. I wish I could put the past behind me and know I am safe, but with anaphylaxis a very real risk every day, I can't do that. That's the difference between PTSD from a traumatic event, and PTSD from food allergies.

I didn't ask for PTSD. I didn't choose OCD. I don't want to live in fear. I just want to feel safe. Every day, I show up and try again. Some days, I do something brave like try a new food or resist the urge to wipe my hands again. Other days, I can't, and that's okay too. Healing doesn't happen all at once. It happens in tiny pieces, little wins. Some days are survival days—and on survival days, it's enough just to get through.

Key Takeaways:

Believe the fear, even if you can't see it. Don't assume a child is overreacting when they avoid food, wipe their hands, or check that someone is still breathing. Trauma teaches the brain to look for danger everywhere. What seems "silly" to you might be survival to them.

Never say, "You'll be fine" or "Just trust me." Those words can feel like pressure or dismissal. Trust doesn't come easily after trauma, especially when things that were meant to be "safe" have caused harm previously. Build trust slowly and show through your actions that safety really matters to you.

Be patient with compulsions. Washing hands multiple times or checking doors might seem excessive, but stopping suddenly can cause panic. Work gently with the child (and qualified health professionals) to find safer alternatives when they're ready.

Respect fears, even if you think they are safe. Don't force a child to do something they are scared of. Don't say "It's fine" and expect them to believe you. Ask what they need to feel safe and let them take it at their pace. Stay close to them so they feel supported.

Don't joke about allergies or hygiene routines. Kids who are living with trauma related to anaphylaxis often feel isolated. Be kind and take it seriously. Separate utensils might seem unnecessary to others, but they can be the difference between eating and not eating at all. Support these needs without question or judgement.

Teach others to stop eye-rolling, sighing, or brushing things off. When people dismiss a child's fears, it confirms the belief that adults don't care or don't get it. Help others around them respond with patience and respect instead of annoyance or sarcasm.

Make the environment feel predictable. Trauma makes the world feel unsafe and unpredictable. Clear routines, honest explanations, and safe zones (like a private eating area or sensory tent) help the child's nervous system calm down.

Allow survival days. Some days, just showing up is a huge win. If the child can't participate, try the new thing or attend the event, don't punish or shame them. Let them know it's okay to take a break and try again another day. Sometimes they might just need to relax and cuddle something quietly.

Celebrate the little wins. Trying one bite, touching a fork, or resisting a compulsion to wash their hands yet again is a huge step. Don't make it a big deal in front of others. Let the child know you noticed, you appreciate how hard it was for them and you're proud of them.

Be someone they can rely on. If you say you'll call, call. If you say the food is dairy free, check it twice. Consistency and reliability are everything. Trauma teaches that safety can disappear in an instant. Prove through your actions that you're one of those people who can be reliable.

Understand that this isn't a choice. No one chooses to live in fear, follow routines they don't want, or panic over mashed potato. This isn't attention-seeking. It's trauma. Every day they fight a battle you can't see, so don't make it harder.

Show compassion, not frustration. Even when it's inconvenient or confusing to you, respond with kindness. Your calm presence can be one of the few things that help a child feel even a little bit safe.

10

Grief: Loss in Many Forms

Grief isn't just about death. It's about change. It's about losing people, routines, and pieces of your life you thought were meant to stay. For me, grief came in waves. It didn't always look the way people expected it to. Sometimes it came with crying. Other times it came with fear or chaos or silence. It often showed up when I didn't even realise it was grief. I thought something was wrong with me, but really, something had been taken from me.

When I was six, my Grandpa died. He was one of the most important people in my life. He wasn't just a grandparent, he was my world. He helped raise me. He was the one who scratched my back when I was upset and held me when I needed comfort. He made me feel safe. He gave me a sense of calm in a life that often felt uncertain. I loved him deeply.

He got sick, and we visited him again and again in hospital. I remember seeing him hooked up to machines, but I didn't really understand what was happening. Adults whispered around me, and I knew something was wrong, but no one said it straight. Then one day, he was just gone. No more visits. No more cuddles. No more back scratches. Gone.

I was only six. I didn't understand grief the way adults do. I actually thought it was a good thing. I was told Grandpa had gone to a better place where there was no pain, and I believed it. I thought we should celebrate that. I felt relieved that he wasn't hurting any more. I thought it was beautiful that we'd see him again one day, so I smiled. I laughed. I was bubbly and boisterous. I didn't realise people were grieving in a different way. Everyone around me was crying, and I couldn't understand why. I thought I was doing the right thing by being happy. I thought I was helping. I remember tickling people who were crying, not to be rude or mean, but because I thought it might cheer them up. I didn't know yet that sometimes people need space for sadness.

My Mum sent me to my sister's place so she could deal with the hospital, care for my Grandma and take care of all the arrangements. I kept jumping from the couch onto the ottoman, laughing, over and over, again and again. I couldn't stop. It was like my body needed to move or I'd explode. I must have done it a hundred times. My sister didn't know what to do with me. She ended up calling Mum and saying, "You need to come and get her." I wasn't misbehaving. I was grieving. I just didn't have the words or understanding yet to know that's what it was.

It was more than a month before I cried. It happened when I was watching the video we had made for his funeral. It struck me that he was gone. He wasn't coming back. For a while, I tried to die so I could go and see him. Mum had to grab my hand when I tried to step out onto the road. I told her I wanted to go see Grandpa, but she explained that he wouldn't want that. He wanted to watch over me and see me enjoying my life. He'd still be there waiting for me when I was older.

After Grandpa died, everything changed. I became terrified of hospitals. They weren't just places with doctors any more. They were places where people disappeared and never came back. My brain started connecting sickness with death. If someone got sick, I thought they were going to die. I couldn't help it. It became this automatic fear that followed me everywhere. My separation anxiety worsened. I didn't want to go to school. I didn't want to leave the car. I didn't want to say goodbye to Mum in case it was the last time. I'd panic at school drop-off. I'd need her to walk me to my classroom at a time when most kids were being more independent. I was scared she'd disappear too, just like Grandpa did.

I didn't just grieve people. I also grieved all the parts of childhood I never got to have. Because of my medical conditions, as I got older, I missed out on birthday parties, sleepovers, camps, and even just eating the same food as everyone else. I watched other kids eat cake and run around while I sat with my special packed lunch. I wanted to join in so badly, but I couldn't, and that hurt in a deep, quiet way.

No one really talks about that kind of grief—the grief of not getting to be a normal kid, but it's real and it builds up. Every time I missed out, it was like another tiny piece of childhood slipped away. Sometimes, the sadness didn't hit me right away. It would come later when I was alone in my room. I'd cry without fully knowing why. It was grief.

I also experienced grief that came from lost opportunities and crushed dreams. When I was younger, I had started learning gymnastics. I loved it. I was becoming better at it too. I was even encouraged to enter a competition. It was such an exciting time for me—preparing for my very first competition. But then, my body let me down. My knees started hurting ... a lot. Walking was painful. We went to the GP who sent me to a specialist. He told me I had hyperflexive joints and that if I kept doing gymnastics, it would only get worse, so I had to stop. I was devastated. I felt depressed and anxious. I thought I'd never be able to do fun physical activities again.

Later on, I discovered aerial silks and lyra. I fell in love with it. I'd go to the park almost daily just to hang off the bars and spin around. I was so happy. And again, I started preparing for a competition. I choreographed my own routine and performed it at a showcase. It was amazing. However, all the extra practice took its toll. My shoulders started hurting badly. After getting an X-ray and ultrasound, we found out I had bursitis in both shoulders and a small groove in my bones where my muscles were supposed to sit, which meant they could easily slip out of place. Just like that, I had to stop aerials too.

That loss hit hard. I grieved all over again, but this time, something different happened. I was sent to an incredible exercise physiologist and physiotherapist—Adam Russell from PRP Health. He referred me to a sports medicine specialist, Dr Martin Smith at QSports. And instead of telling me "You can't do aerials anymore," Dr Smith and Adam said something amazing. They said they'd help me build strength in my arms so that one day I *can* return to aerials. That gave me so much hope. I can't wait to go back to doing what I love. I can't thank them enough for their unwavering support.

When my dad died of cancer, I felt a different type of grief. It was complicated. He hadn't been a safe person in my life. He hadn't raised me or supported me in the way I needed, but he was still my dad. His death stirred up all kinds of emotions—sadness, anger, confusion, and guilt. I didn't know how to feel. Part of me grieved the relationship we never got to have. I felt like there were things that would never be said, hugs that would never happen, memories that would never be made. I wanted to jump on a plane and leave my camp to go see him without anyone knowing, using money I had saved. I planned my journey, how much an uber would cost, but I kept remembering that Dad said he wanted me to go to the camp, and he had paid for it. Sadly, he died while I was on camp. I was so sad, Mum came and collected me. People often don't understand that grief can exist even for people who hurt you or weren't there, but it can. Grief doesn't always make sense.

Grief followed me into school too. I'd space out and forget what I was doing. Teachers didn't always understand. Sometimes they thought I was being lazy or not listening, but I wasn't. I was hurting, and I didn't know how to say it.

The recent death of my guinea pig, my therapy pet, my friend, was really traumatic. The grief was indescribable. Now it is really hard to let myself love another animal.

Even now, grief comes in waves. It can be triggered by anything—a smell, a song, a place, a colour. Sometimes it hits out of nowhere. One moment I'll be fine, the next I'll feel heavy and tired and teary. It lives deep in my chest like a quiet ache. Over time, I've found ways to carry it better.

Writing has helped. Creating my pixie characters and their stories gives my feelings somewhere to go. I can write about things happening to someone else, not me. Helping others has helped too. When I turn my pain into purpose, it feels a little less pointless. Most importantly, I've learned that it's okay to grieve what never was, not just what ended: the childhood I didn't have, the people I hoped to become closer with and the 'normal' moments I missed.

Giving children the opportunity to feel their emotions is really important. Acknowledge their grief. Allow them to feel the sadness, the loss and then help them move on.

Key Takeaways:

Don't assume grief always looks like tears. Watch for grief in behaviour, not just words. Some kids laugh, run, fidget, or even seem cheerful. It might be their way of coping or protecting themselves from overwhelming emotions. A child bouncing off furniture, zoning out at school, or refusing to separate from a parent might be grieving in a way they can't explain.

Let children be free to express themselves. Writing, drawing, movement, play, music, and silence are all valid ways to process emotions. There's no one "right" way to grieve. Sometimes kids need to move or be doing an activity when they talk about the hard stuff. Allow them the freedom to do that, rather than making them sit and make eye contact.

Help them feel understood, not judged. Avoid calling them "overdramatic," "lazy," or "disruptive." What looks like misbehaviour might be pain they don't know how to explain.

Explain grief in honest, age-appropriate ways. Gently explain what death or loss means so children don't feel confused when others are sad.

Validate all types of grief—not just the loss of people. Kids might grieve missed parties, cancelled plans, sports they can't play any more, or the childhood experiences they didn't get to have.

Don't rush them to "move on." Grief can last a long time and return without warning when triggered. Be patient. Let them know it's okay if sad feelings come back months or years later.

Give extra support when separation anxiety shows up. Fear of losing someone else is understandable in grieving kids who have lost someone they love, through family breakdown or death. Offer consistent reassurance, predictable routines, and safe goodbyes.

Support complicated grief, even for people who weren't safe or close. Kids can still grieve relationships they never had or wished they had. That grief is real and deserves kindness.

Acknowledge lost dreams and crushed hopes. Kids can grieve missed opportunities or being withdrawn from activities they love. I was devastated when I was told I couldn't do gymnastics. Let kids talk about the things they miss doing. If possible, work with professionals to adapt or find new ways to help them keep going with what they love.

Let grief be felt. Create a sensory space where kids feel safe to feel the hard stuff, then gently guide them toward healing when they're ready.

Be the adult who brings hope. Help kids move forward after the pain in practical ways like having fun times, giving kids hope that the future will be better.

11

Depression: When the World Feels Too Much

Depression didn't start with sadness. It started with feeling like I was invisible. Like I didn't belong. Like I was too much for people. Like I should hide myself so no one had to deal with me. I used to tell myself, "They'll be happier without me." "I'll be nice and disappear." "I don't deserve help." These thoughts didn't just come once. They were the same thoughts that came again and again when things got hard. I felt ashamed for needing more help than other kids. I hated that I couldn't do things other kids could do. I hated that I wasn't 'normal'. A lot of people say that people with medical needs seem happy enough but a lot of the time we put on a happy, funny mask to hide our discomfort from you because we think you don't deserve to see our pain, that we'll be a burden if we let you in.

When I was told I needed medication, it made me feel like something was 'wrong' in my brain. I felt like I was broken and I wasn't safe—not even in my own mind. When I had side effects to medication, like seeing horrific images or getting hallucinations, it made things even worse. It confirmed my fear that my brain was unsafe. I felt like I couldn't even trust myself. It scared me. I already felt like I was a burden. I believed other people would finally have peace if I just wasn't here. I didn't want to die. I just didn't want to keep feeling the way I did.

There were days I wanted to lash out, scream, smash something, break things, but I also felt guilty for feeling like that. I held it all in: the anger, the shame and the frustration. I didn't want people to see that side of me. I wanted to seem okay, even when I wasn't. That just made things feel heavier. I constantly put myself under pressure to act okay, to be someone I wasn't. I was under so much pressure, and I didn't have the words to explain it. I didn't even understand it all myself.

People tried to help, but their strategies didn't work for me. Things like "write your worries down" or "take a deep breath" didn't help, especially after I'd been through something traumatic like anaphylaxis. Those ideas felt like putting a tiny Band-Aid over a broken bone. They didn't touch what I was really feeling. What helped more was being truly listened to. Having a support team was crucial. Talking to someone who had been through something similar really helped me. Colouring until I was calm was a great strategy at school when I had reached my meltdown point. Taking short breaks was great to give my brain time to reset. Mindfulness helped, but only in a way that worked for me, not just the way people expected. Sometimes talking to my imaginary friends helped. Writing helped too. It gave me a way to express things I couldn't say out loud.

Having NVLD made things even harder. I often didn't know what people meant. I couldn't tell if they were serious or joking. I'd take things the wrong way or feel awkward and confused. I spent so much time trying to work out what I was supposed to do or say. It made me second guess myself constantly. And when I already felt broken or like I didn't belong, this just made it worse. I told myself again, "They'll be happier without me." "I'll just disappear." "There's something wrong with me." I even cut myself out of a photo with my friends once, because I didn't feel like I belonged in it. That's how strong those feelings were.

In Year 4, I missed a lot of school. I had so many medical appointments. I saw the endocrinologist for my precocious puberty and had my three-monthly Lucrin injections. I had to see the gastroenterologist for my chronic constipation, the urologist for my small, overactive bladder, the dermatologist, the allergist, the neurologist, the psychiatrist, the psychologist and the occupational therapist. Many of these were weekly or fortnightly. It felt like appointment after appointment, and not much time for just being a kid. Eventually, Mum made a decision. She stopped many of the appointments and used the money to take me to fun places and do enjoyable things. Giving me some joy again helped a lot.

However, the pressure didn't stop. Because I'd missed so much, my teacher pulled Mum aside one day. There was a school showcase coming up and I hadn't finished some of the work. The teacher asked if I could finish it over the weekend. Mum said, "Sure, no problem." But she didn't know how much was missing. It felt like I was being asked to do an entire term's work in two days. I worked from 9 to 5 on Saturday and again on Sunday but I still couldn't finish it all. I was exhausted. Mum told me to stop and said she would speak to the teacher on Monday.

That Monday, I was pulled out of class to work with the teacher aide. I was so tired that the aide ended up doing most of the work.

It didn't feel like anyone cared if I understood. It felt like they just wanted something to show. The pressure to look like I was keeping up was more important than actually learning. That happened again when I was in an online school. They told Mum to "forget about learning and just do the assessments". Mum said, "Isn't that backwards? Isn't learning the most important thing?" It didn't make sense. I didn't stay at that school for long. I went back to learning at home with Mum, at my pace, where learning was about understanding, not rushing or ticking boxes.

Even now, I still carry depression with me. It hasn't disappeared, but I've survived it before. I've learned what helps. I've learned that when those thoughts come like "I don't deserve help" or "I should disappear", I don't have to listen to them. They're not true. I am still here. And that counts for something.

Key Takeaways:

Notice the signs beyond sadness. Depression can look like shame, fear, withdrawal, or feeling like a burden. Look for changes in how they see themselves, not just if they seem "sad."

Don't downplay dark thoughts. If a child says things like "They'd be happier without me" or "I should disappear," take it seriously. Those thoughts are real and scary, even if they're said quietly or with a smile.

Understand the extra weight of neurodivergence and illness. Conditions like NVLD, chronic pain, and medical trauma can make depression more complex. These kids often struggle to explain what they're feeling.

Do not expect quick catch-up after absences. Missing school for medical appointments adds stress. Don't pile on too much pressure to catch up on missed work. Focus on helping them understand missed concepts, not just complete tasks for the sake of it. Make it worthwhile. Reduce the workload if possible.

Prioritise learning over deadlines. It's not about ticking boxes or making things look good for a school showcase. Support understanding, not perfection. Celebrate effort, not just outcomes.

Avoid one-size-fits-all strategies. Telling kids to "write it down" or "breathe deeply" doesn't always help, especially after trauma. Offer tools that match the child, not the textbook.

Take concerns about medication seriously. If a child says a medication is making them feel unsafe or causing side effects, listen and believe them. Don't brush it off. They are the ones experiencing the issue, not you. You have no idea what is going on inside their brain or body.

Be the listener, not the fixer. Sometimes what helps most is someone who just listens and stays. You don't have to have all the answers. Just be there for them.

Build a support team. Include people with lived experience if you can. Kids feel seen when someone understands what they've been through. Make sure the team uses a consistent approach, so there is no conflicting advice.

Schedule in joy and rest. Make time for calming activities like colouring, painting, writing, music, dance, using sensory fidgets or talking to imaginary friends. These aren't distractions, they're coping tools.

Allow brain breaks. Short breaks can give overwhelmed minds a chance to reset. Don't underestimate how powerful a few quiet or active minutes can be. I developed my Pixie Challenge Cards so I could use them to have little breaks when I needed to reset. They really helped me.

Let them be real. Kids don't have to be perfect to deserve care. Let them show their true feelings, even anger or confusion, without shame.

Recognise survival as a win. Don't wait for a child to be "better" to be proud of them. Let them know just getting through tough days is something worth celebrating.

12

Suicidal Thoughts: The Shame of Needing Help

Most suicide support focuses on teenagers, but I want to highlight that depression and suicidal ideation can start a lot younger than that. I was nine, not a teenager, and I had already tried to give up. For me, depression and suicide are not the same. I can be depressed but say 'no' to thoughts of suicide. I can cry, be upset, be low, but not be suicidal. Sometimes, I can be both. I wanted to distinguish the two different experiences as two different chapters because I think that I need to highlight this. We need to consider the mental health of young children a lot more. Kids like me, the quiet ones, aren't always noticed. Sometimes, by the time people do notice, it's already gotten really bad. I wasn't acting out. I wasn't naughty. I was the quiet, well-behaved, conscientious kid in the classroom, but I was struggling. Just because I wasn't loud or disruptive didn't mean I was okay.

I wasn't just dealing with one thing. I had Generalised Anxiety Disorder, PTSD, depression and then suicidal thoughts by age 9. I had medical trauma. I had drug reactions, including one that made me hallucinate. I had bowel and bladder issues that were humiliating. I had been diagnosed with NVLD, sensory processing difficulties, executive functioning problems, social communication issues, visual-spatial deficits, and more. I had allergies, anaphylaxis, asthma and severe eczema. I had precocious puberty and had been having 3-monthly injections for that. I also had adverse reactions to the medicine for my 'scrambled brain'. My body wasn't working right. My brain wasn't working right. It was all too much to handle. I wanted out. I wanted it all to end so I could be at peace and so could everyone else.

When I was nine years old, I tried committing suicide with a knife in my chest. I knew exactly what I was doing. It wasn't attention-seeking. I wanted to die. I wanted to stop feeling how I was feeling. I wanted to stop existing. I didn't want to wake up. I didn't want to go on. The main reason was to help others not have to deal with me. I felt like everyone would be better off without me. They'd have peace. I thought, "I'll be nice and hide from my friends, so they don't have to deal with me." After all, they didn't deserve to have to be around me. I didn't feel like I mattered. I felt invisible. I didn't feel like anyone understood what was happening for me.

On the outside, I wore my "I'm fine" mask, but I wasn't fine. I was distressed. I was overwhelmed. I was done. Even when I wasn't crying on the outside, I felt like I was crying inside. I had already stopped taking the epilepsy medicine which caused the suicidal ideations in the first place, but the thoughts continued for years. I was ashamed. Obviously, there was something 'wrong' in my head – that's why I needed the medicine in the first place, right? I often had to reframe my thoughts. For instance, whenever I got hurt, I would think, "Well that's okay. You deserved it." I would have to reframe it to, "Um, no, that's not right. I didn't deserve that. I am not going to harm myself."

Even after the medicine had stopped, I didn't want to be here any more. When I was diagnosed with NVLD, I tried running away from the psychologist. I thought about dying in all sorts of ways. Apart from the knife, I also tried to jump out of the car when Mum was doing 80 kph. I imagined how I could jump off a bridge and worked out how I could get a taxi to get there so Mum didn't have to take me. I imagined using my necklace to burn or choke myself and tried to choke myself on my retainers. Lots of things triggered me long after the medicine had stopped. Even today, when I am unstacking the dishwasher, I can find myself unknowingly placing the knife over my heart until I snap out of it and realise what I am doing.

I wanted to escape my life, so I tried to hide. I hid in the library. I hid in the bathroom. I thought I was doing people a favour by staying out of the way. I felt like a burden. I felt like a failure. I couldn't keep up. I couldn't do what was expected. I would pretend to go in the bathroom or the shower by shutting the door. I would roleplay and feel my 'inexistence' from the house. I tried to listen in to see if my Mum and Grandma would share something bad about me when they thought I was gone, to get their real thoughts about me, to see if they actually wanted me to be in their lives.

People would say to me, "Why haven't you done this strategy?" "Have you taken your medicine?" "Have you brushed your hair?" "Are you ready yet?" I just wanted to be left alone. I just wanted it all to stop. I couldn't do that. I had lost almost all of my energy just trying to survive. People said to take a deep breath—but that doesn't help when you've had anaphylaxis. Breathing is the trauma. Being told to write your worries and put them in a box didn't help when the worry was still there all the time. I didn't want more strategies. I wanted people to actually see what was going on for me.

I had no control over my life or my body. I was angry. I was frustrated. I wanted to lash out. I cornered Mum one day, trying to hurt her, but then I was overwhelmed by guilt and shame. I didn't know what to do. It wasn't just normal anger. It was like I was in a bubble and my thoughts were all-consuming to punch her, kick her, try to kill her, anything that would have her be scared or screaming for me to stop. My brain was snickering. I couldn't just snap out of it. I felt incapable of controlling my body, my thoughts and what I was doing. I felt like all the muscles and bones in my body were not mine, uncontrolled and I felt scared for both Mum and me. I felt like I was in an anger zone that I couldn't snap out of until I hurt her. She had done nothing wrong.

My medication changed the way my brain thought. When I was on the medication, I would hope the tree above would release a seedpod, pinecone, etc. to go through Mum's car windshield and kill her, or hurt her at least. My thoughts were uncontrollable. I felt so bad. Even after the medicine stopped, I would still be plagued by the thoughts.. I still sometimes think about Mum dying and also suicide. This has impacted my self-esteem. People call me a lovely girl but I often wonder if they knew the past information about me and what happened, would they still believe that? Even though it wasn't my fault that the medicines caused that, I still feel horrible about it. This has led to fear of being around people in case my brain goes into that zone again. It probably won't, but I do fear being out of control of myself.

School made it worse. Teachers didn't always listen to the professionals. They ignored my psychiatrist's advice. I was expected to catch up on all my missed schoolwork even when I hadn't been well. I was seated next to a bully to 'work it out'. I was put next to the teacher's desk so she could 'help' me, but that just made me feel worse. I felt like I was being watched all the time. I was even suspended and threatened with expulsion because of my suicidal ideation after I told the teacher aide I felt like running away. That made everything worse. I didn't need punishment. I needed support. It led me to feel that I wasn't safe to share about my experiences and I needed to pretend everything was okay.

Some things did help. My team of Mum, Grandma, my psychiatrist, psychologist, OT, and some teachers, worked together. They created a document outlining all my health issues, the impact they had on me and strategies that could be used to support me. My psychiatrist created a contextualised anxiety scale for me. Normally, people know the blue, green, yellow, orange and red zones, but she explained that for me, who lived constantly in the orange and red zones, when something happened, I would shoot right off the chart into the catastrophic zone. For me, everything was life and death ... catastrophic. If I eat this, am I going to die? Grandpa died. Is Mum going to die too? The purple zone.

My support team also used the Iceberg Strategy. On the sheet my Mum created, I would write, at the tip of the iceberg, what behaviour I was doing or what I was saying. Under the water, where the main part of the iceberg lurked, I would write all the other things I was thinking or worrying about that nobody knew about. Then, at the bottom of the page, I would have to think about which calming strategy I could use to help get me back into the 'green zone' (or as close as I could get to it) to be able to focus again. One day, Mum had to stop me from writing under the iceberg. I had filled up the whole iceberg as well as all up both sides of the page. It was as if the one trigger had opened all the little boxes in my brain containing all the other trauma, and once one lock was opened, they all snapped open again. She helped me close those box lids and redirected me back to what I needed to do. That strategy helped me understand why I often felt like exploding.

Another strategy that helped was that each morning, I would meet with my teacher aide. She had created a special notebook, just for me, which contained positive affirmations. We had a chance to chat about how I was feeling that day. It was great until the day I told her I felt like running away and she reported it to the office, which led to me being suspended for 3 days. That was definitely not helpful. I didn't understand what I had done wrong. It also meant I felt I could no longer trust her. Again, I had said the wrong thing.

Talking to a lady with lived experience of chronic illness, pain and mental health conditions helped me a lot. We just went to the beach and sat and chatted while Mum sat away and read her book. She shared with me some strategies and tips that helped her, but most importantly, it made me feel less alone. Just knowing that she understood what it was like was very reassuring. That is what I try to bring to the children I meet—someone who has 'been there' and understands what it's like to struggle every day.

Mindfulness and colouring helped. Sensory fidgets helped, especially my own soft, silent fidgets. I didn't like the hard, clicky, plastic fidgets. They could be very irritating for me and those around me. I really wanted soft ones, like a therapy pet, but I couldn't find any, so I developed my own. ASMR helped. Watching reels and YouTube shorts from other people who had struggled helped me. Seeing that I wasn't the only one made a difference. Seeing people recover gave me hope.

Writing my children's books helped me. It helped me make sense of what I was feeling. It helped me believe that maybe my stories could help someone else. My business gave me purpose. It gave me a reason to keep going.

Obviously, everyone's experiences with depression and suicidal ideations are different. Everyone's reasons are different. Everyone's road to recovery is different. I hope these insights will help you better understand any young people you have at home or ones you work with. The most important thing is to encourage openness and honesty and be there to listen and walk with them on the journey if they choose to include you.

Key Takeaways:

Don't assume suicidal thoughts only happen to teenagers. Depression and suicidal ideation can start very young. Children as young as six or seven can feel hopeless. Listen carefully, even if they're younger than you'd expect.

Believe kids when they say they're not okay. If a child says they're struggling or wants to disappear, don't ignore it or brush it off. Take them seriously every single time. Their words might be the only warning sign.

Never punish a child for talking about suicidal thoughts. Suicidal ideation is not bad behaviour. It's a sign of distress. Respond with compassion, not consequences. Shame makes it worse. Understanding helps them feel safe enough to open up again.

Speak positively about the child, even when they're not in the room. Children often overhear things (especially when people think they are asleep). If they hear adults saying kind, hopeful things about them, it builds self-worth. If they hear blame or frustration, it can increase shame.

Only use strategies once the child feels safe. Don't try to teach coping strategies when they are in meltdown or panicking. Wait until their body and brain have calmed down. That's when learning and connection can happen. In the red or purple zones, logic isn't working. Breathing strategies only help after they've come back to a calmer state. Until then, focus on safety and staying close.

Use deep pressure and gentle humour to bring calm. Firm hugs (if they're okay with it), weighted blankets, tickles, playing 'sausage roll' or telling jokes can shift a child out of panic. Using different senses activates different parts of the brain and distracts them from their other thoughts.

Recognise how medical trauma, anxiety, and sensory overload can build up. It's never "just" anxiety or "just" trauma. Everything adds up. The more pressure a child is under, the more likely they are to reach breaking point.

Take away extra instructions and demands when they're overwhelmed. When a child is struggling, piling on tasks or expectations can push them further down (or closer to the edge of the cliff). Give space, quiet, and time to just be. Downtime is essential. Let them know you are there if they need you. Sometimes doing a little chore of theirs relieves some of the pressure. When I was really struggling, unstacking the dishwasher was hard because it was triggering my memories, so Mum put away the cutlery and I did the rest.

Look at the whole child, not just one diagnosis. Make sure all professionals are working together and keeping the whole child at the centre. Medical professionals need to consider all aspects of the child and be aware of everything that is going on for that child, not just focus on their field. The dermatologists needed to understand everything else I had to deal with to understand why it was so hard to do my creams.

Use tools like the Iceberg Strategy to understand what's hidden. What you see, like outbursts or silence, is only the tip. Beneath that might be fear, pain, shame, exhaustion, trauma. Always look deeper.

Use quiet, calming voice tones to settle a distressed child. Speak slowly and gently. Lower your pitch at the end of each sentence, like you're calming a scared horse: "You're okay. You're safe. I'm here." Tone matters as much as words. Kids with neurodiversity often have difficulty interpreting tone, but volume can impact us. Loud voices seem angry even when they are not.

Let kids express big feelings in their own way. Not all kids talk easily. Some draw, write, or play out their feelings. Let them use whatever method helps them feel heard.

If you are worried, keep them close. If you have concerns that your child may be really struggling, be unobtrusive, but keep them close. Watch television together, draw or colour together, play a game together or just sit with them while they play on their device. Beware letting them hide away alone in their room.

Allow movement during tough conversations. Sitting still can make hard topics harder. Let them bounce, pace, or fidget while you talk. Movement helps me regulate my emotions.

Give them a consistent support person they can rely on. Having the same teacher aide or adult each morning builds safety and trust. It's one less thing to worry about in a world that often feels chaotic.

Work as a team that truly listens to the child. Every person on the team, parents, teachers and health professionals, needs to be on the same page. Most importantly, the child's voice must be part of that team too.

Create a space where honesty is safe. Let kids talk about scary feelings without fear of being in trouble. Show them it's okay to be sad, scared, or overwhelmed. Let them know they'll still be accepted and loved.

If you are concerned about your child's mental health and fear they are a danger to themselves, seek qualified medical advice or ring for an ambulance. In Australia, ring 000.

13

Body Image and EDNOS

I was never officially diagnosed with an eating disorder or a body image disorder, but psychologists have said they think I was struggling with both. Looking back, the signs were all there, but because I didn't have a formal diagnosis, people didn't always take it seriously. It was easier for others to brush it off as a phase or dismiss it because I didn't have anorexia or bulimia. I wasn't throwing up, so I felt I didn't need as much help as other kids. I wasn't worthy of help. I wondered if they thought I was just being dramatic. Inside, it was affecting every part of my day.

It's hard to explain what it feels like unless you've been through it. When people think of eating disorders, they often imagine someone refusing to eat or always trying to lose weight. But it's not always that obvious. For me, it was about control, fear, and constant comparison. It was about a million tiny thoughts that built up over time until I couldn't escape them. Even when no one else noticed, I was always aware of how I looked, how I felt, and how I compared to everyone else.

Social media had a weird role in all of this. For some people, it can make everything worse—and I get that. However, for me, it actually helped, at least in the later stages. I made the choice to follow positive influencers. I didn't want to be constantly surrounded by photos of perfect bodies and fake smiles. Instead, I found real people: other teens who were honest about their struggles, their healing, and the ups and downs they were facing. They helped me feel less alone. They didn't pretend everything was perfect, and that honesty mattered.

I found people my age going through the same things, but also healthy fitness people talking about body image and EDNOS (Eating Disorder Not Otherwise Specified). They were just people trying to survive the same kinds of thoughts I had. That connection gave me space to breathe. They got it. They understood that the problem wasn't just about food or weight. It was deeper than that. It was about how we saw ourselves, how we judged our bodies, and how afraid we were of losing control.

One of the biggest triggers for me was how my body changed throughout the day. My medications caused bloating, and I'd watch my body shift in real time. It wasn't in my head. It was real. I could see my belly grow as the day went on. Sometimes it felt like I couldn't trust my own body any more. I didn't know what it was going to look like from one hour to the next. I could start the day feeling okay, and by the afternoon, my clothes would feel tight, my belly would feel swollen, and my brain would spiral. The bloating from medication wasn't something I could control, but I still blamed myself for it. Even though I *knew* it was from medication, even though I *knew* it was normal, it still felt like a personal failure every time I saw a new bump or roll. I didn't want people to judge me. I wanted them to understand that I wasn't fat, it was just that the medicine made me feel bloated.

My posture didn't help. Because of chronic pain, I often slouched or sat in weird positions, and that made my belly crease in ways that looked like rolls. I'd look down and panic. I'd squeeze those spots to check if they were real, and that only made me feel worse.

I watched my belly obsessively, not just in mirrors, but everywhere. I would look in car windows, reflections in screens, shadows, shop windows ... anything that showed my outline. I couldn't stop. I would scan my stomach, checking for changes. I would turn to the side and press down on my waistband to see if the skin folded. I wanted to be flat, completely flat. Any curve made me feel sick. It wasn't just about my stomach. I compared my whole body—my fingers, my arms, my cheeks, even my smile.

My face became another source of stress. It looked round to me, no matter what anyone said. Even when people told me I looked like a skeleton, that I was too thin, all I could focus on was how fat I thought my face looked. The compliments didn't make me feel better. They just confused me. If people said I was all bones, why did I still feel huge? It didn't make sense, but that's the thing about disordered thinking: it doesn't listen to logic.

Old photos became another obsession. I would scroll through pictures of myself when I was 10 or 12 and compare them to how I looked now. I would try to figure out where the changes had happened. Was it my hips? My belly? My face? I studied every image like it was a puzzle I had to solve. I compared myself to my Mum too. I would stand next to her and try to guess if I was half her size. I was scared of getting to her size—not because there was anything wrong with her, but because in my mind, that meant I had failed. I had let go. I was out of control.

Being weighed was one of the hardest things. It completely controlled how I felt about myself. If I stepped on the scale and saw 49.2kg, I felt okay, but if it said 49.4kg, everything changed. I'd panic. I'd start doing the math—what if it went up 0.1kg more? What if I hit 49.5kg? What if I hit 50kg? That number, 50, was terrifying. In my mind, 50kg meant 'fat'. It meant I had crossed a line. It didn't matter that I was still healthy. It didn't matter that the doctors said I was fine. That number felt like a failure.

The worst part was that I *knew* it was irrational. I knew it didn't make sense, but I couldn't stop feeling that way. Even now, I look at gym girls I admire who are 60kg or more, and I think they look amazing. They are strong, confident and fit, but back then, none of that mattered. I couldn't apply that kindness to myself.

I started tracking everything. I tracked my BMI, my body fat percentage, and my waist-to-hip ratio. I hid a tape measure in the bathroom and used it secretly to take measurements. I'd search up online calculators and plug in the numbers. I did this regularly, sometimes more than once a day. I felt like I needed to check, to be sure, but no matter what the results said, I always felt worse afterward. Even when the ratios didn't make sense (because they often don't when you're still in puberty), I still believed them. The calculators would say I was overweight because of my hip measurements, even though my doctors told me I was perfectly healthy. It didn't matter. The numbers became more important to me than the truth.

Clothes shopping became another trigger. Changing rooms became a place of dread. I'd bring in a stack of clothes, hoping something would fit. I'd try on size after size and want to scream when nothing felt right. I stood under harsh lights, picking apart every curve and crease. I just wanted to go home. I stopped buying clothes that were size 10 or 12, even if I liked them. I only wanted to wear sizes 6 or 8. If something said "small" or "extra small," I felt good. If it said "medium" or "large," I felt gross. If I could still fit into kids' clothes, I would feel proud. I tied my worth to the size on the label. I know that sizing is different across brands, that some clothes are tighter or looser depending on the style, but it didn't matter. If the tag didn't match what I wanted, I didn't feel okay. I'd rather not buy anything than admit I needed a bigger size. Sometimes I would buy the small size and then not be able to wear it because it hurt my stomach.

I became obsessed with other people's sizes too. I'd look at their tags when they were hanging out of their shirts or pants. I needed to know what size they wore. I'd compare it to mine and decide if I was "okay" that day. If someone my age wore a bigger size, I felt relieved. If they wore a smaller size, I'd spiral.

All of this became a full-time job in my head. Even when I was doing other things, my thoughts were on my body, how I looked, how I felt, what I ate, whether I was okay, gaining weight or losing control. It was exhausting. It took so much energy to keep up the appearance of being fine when inside I was fighting all these negative thoughts.

The worst part was that I wasn't the type of kid people expected to be struggling. I wasn't loud or angry or rebellious. I wasn't "acting out." I was the quiet, well-behaved, conscientious kid in the classroom. I got my work done. I followed all the rules. I smiled at the right times. I looked fine on the outside, but that didn't mean I was fine on the inside.

These thoughts didn't just switch off when school ended. I carried them everywhere: into my friendships, into my family life, into moments that should have been fun. I remember once being at a sleepover and secretly checking my reflection in the microwave door while everyone else was watching a movie. I didn't want anyone to notice, but I couldn't help it. I just needed to know if my stomach looked bigger than earlier.

I hated going to events where people took photos. I'd feel okay before the picture was taken, but once I saw it, I'd pick it apart. I'd zoom in on my arms, my belly, my face. I'd delete pictures of myself. I didn't want memories if they showed me looking "wrong."

Then there was food. I didn't restrict foods in the traditional sense, but food became something I feared. I would worry about every bite. I'd wonder if it would make me gain weight. I would second-guess myself constantly. Sometimes I wouldn't eat what I actually wanted. I'd pick something I thought was 'safe' instead. But even the 'safe' choices didn't feel safe. I still felt guilty afterward, like I was losing control.

It has taken me a long time to admit that this was disordered eating. I used to tell myself it wasn't that bad, that other people had it worse. Just because I wasn't hospitalised or underweight, doesn't mean I wasn't hurting. Disordered eating doesn't always look the way people expect. Just because it didn't fit a neat diagnosis didn't mean it wasn't real.

Even when I wanted to get better, I didn't know what that meant. Did it mean eating more? Accepting my body? Not caring what the scales said? All of those things felt impossible, but I kept going, not because I felt brave, but because I was tired of feeling like a prisoner in my own body.

Sometimes I still think about going back and checking again, doing the measurements and calculating the numbers, but I know it would only make me feel terrible, especially now, when I'm dealing with medication side effects, bloating and hormonal changes. It would be a disaster. I don't want to go back there. I've worked too hard to start all over again.

Now, I try to treat my body with more kindness. I try not to punish it for changing. I remind myself that bloating is not failure, that body fat is not a flaw, that I am not defined by a clothing label or a number on a scale.

Key Takeaways:

Don't assume someone is okay just because they seem fine on the outside. Quiet, well-behaved kids might be struggling silently.

Avoid commenting on weight, size, diet or appearance. Even if you think it's a compliment, you don't know how they will interpret what you say.

Don't pressure kids to be weighed. If you must for medical reasons, explain it kindly and share the number if they want to know with a positive comment and smile while you discuss it. Understand that even small weight changes can feel massive to someone who is struggling. Be gentle.

Never push someone to try on clothes. I find trying on clothes in shops absolutely exhausting. Sometimes it is best to buy the clothes and take them home for the child to try in their own safe space. Labels like "large" or "14" can carry big emotional weight. Explain that a size 16 kids is nowhere near a size 16 in adult clothes. I thought I was really fat because I was needing a 16, but my Mum was size 16.

Help kids build worth beyond their body. Notice their internal character. Comment on their kindness, honesty, integrity, creativity, bravery and strength.

Be careful with food language. Avoid saying things like, "You don't need that" or "You're eating too much" or "Are you still hungry?" unless it's a serious health concern. Even then, phrase it gently, with love and understanding.

If a child opens up about body image or disordered eating thoughts, believe them. Don't dismiss it as a phase or because you think they are just following social media trends.

Encourage professional support. Let them know you're there for them, no matter what, but if they need help, seek advice from qualified medical practitioners.

Most of all, be kind every day. They might be fighting a battle you can't see. If you feel comfortable, comment on something positive about their appearance that isn't related to their body like, "I love your nail polish! It suits you so well." Make sure it's not about weight or waist. It makes us feel like we are valuable not just for the way our body looks, but how we treat our body.

SECTION TWO

Neurodiversity

14

What Is NVLD? – A Timeline of Understanding

When I was diagnosed with NVLD (Non-Verbal Learning Disorder), Mum and I didn't just stop at the diagnosis. We needed to understand what it meant. Why was school so hard? Why did I get so confused in social situations, struggle with directions, get overwhelmed by sounds, and take everything people said so literally? We read everything we could get our hands on. Some of it was hard to understand, but we kept going. What we found was that NVLD has been talked about for decades, in fact over 50 years, but a lot of special education teachers, psychologists and medical specialists have never heard of it. Here is a short summary of the timeline of NVLD research.

1960s–1970s: Rourke Notices Something Different

It all started in the 1960s with a Canadian neuropsychologist named Byron Rourke. He began to see a strange but consistent pattern in some of the children he assessed. These kids could talk a lot and had great vocabularies. They did well in areas like reading and remembering facts. But at the same time, they were struggling with everyday things like riding a bike, copying shapes, understanding social cues, and solving visual puzzles.

Dr. Rourke realised this wasn't just a coincidence. He believed these children had a type of learning disorder that hadn't been named yet. He called it "non-verbal learning disabilities," or NVLD. Over time, he developed a model to explain it. He believed it came from problems in the right hemisphere of the brain, especially in the white matter that helps the brain organise and process information about space, distance, and the non-verbal world around us (Rourke, 1989; Rourke, 1995).

This was one of the first times someone had clearly described a learning profile where verbal language skills were strong, but non-verbal areas like visual-spatial thinking, motor coordination, and social skills were weak. Rourke's work became the foundation for how NVLD was understood in future decades.

1980s–1990s: Expanding the Research and Seeing the Pattern

During the 1980s and 1990s, Dr. Rourke continued to study NVLD. He found that it affected much more than just academic tasks. It also caused problems with coordination (like handwriting or using scissors), mathematical reasoning, social interactions, and emotional regulation.

Researchers noticed that many of these kids had a big gap between their verbal IQ and performance IQ. They could explain things with words really well but struggled with patterns, puzzles, and problem-solving that relied on visual skills. That gap became one of the signs of NVLD in assessments (Rourke & Tsatsanis, 2000).

Other experts started to write about the emotional toll NVLD took on kids. Because these children seemed bright and articulate, adults often assumed they should be doing better, but these children were often confused, anxious, and overwhelmed. Nobody could understand why.

2000s–2010s: Confusion and Misunderstanding

By the 2000s, NVLD was more widely known in educational and psychological circles, but it still wasn't in the DSM (Diagnostic and Statistical Manual of Mental Disorders), which is the main book doctors use to make diagnoses.

Some researchers questioned whether NVLD was a real condition or just part of other things like autism spectrum disorder (ASD) or ADHD. Others believed NVLD was its own separate disorder and needed proper recognition (Fine et al., 2013).

The name itself caused confusion. People heard "non-verbal" and assumed it meant a child couldn't speak, which is not true at all. Most people with NVLD are extremely verbal. In fact, it's one of our biggest strengths.

It was during this time that more people started calling for NVLD to be studied properly and defined more clearly. Researchers like Semrud-Clikeman, Volden, and Mammarella started publishing more detailed studies about how NVLD affects different areas of development (Volden & Sagvolden, 2011; Mammarella & Cornoldi, 2014).

2016: The NVLD Project Begins

In 2016, there was a huge step forward in the NVLD community. The NVLD Project was launched in the United States by a parent who wanted to create more awareness after seeing her own child struggle.

The NVLD Project did three major things. It raised awareness by collecting stories from people with NVLD. It funded brain research to understand NVLD better and it worked toward getting NVLD included in the DSM.

They partnered with researchers at Columbia University Medical Center to study children's brains using MRIs. These studies found real neurological differences in the white matter of kids with NVLD, especially in the areas responsible for visual-spatial processing and social understanding (Margolis et al., 2020; Peterson et al., 2021).

This was big news. It proved that NVLD isn't just a learning style or quirk. It's a neurological condition based on how the brain is wired.

2018: My Diagnosis

In 2018, I was nine years old and struggling in lots of ways. People around me were guessing what was going on. Some professionals thought I might have autism because of how I struggled with social communication. I often missed social cues, didn't know when I'd said the wrong thing, and felt confused in conversations.

But I also had other difficulties. I struggled with directions and had no internal map so I got lost all the time, even going from one class to the next. I couldn't copy things from the board easily. My handwriting was messy, and I got lost in visual tasks. I had executive function difficulties like organising my time, remembering steps, and planning ahead. I also took things very literally and worried when people used sarcasm or jokes I didn't understand.

My psychiatrist said I didn't meet the criteria for ASD. Instead, she explained that I had all the features of NVLD. Back then, everything I was experiencing could be explained by NVLD, which included visual-spatial issues *and* executive function, social skills, sensory processing, and literal thinking.

Getting that diagnosis changed everything. It helped me and my family understand why things felt so hard. It didn't fix the struggles, but it gave us the tools to start managing them with more support and understanding.

2020–2023: Changing the Name to DVSD

In 2020, the researchers from the NVLD Project submitted a formal proposal to have NVLD included in the DSM, but they didn't use the same name. Instead, they called it Developmental Visual-Spatial Disorder (DVSD) (Cornoldi et al., 2022).

Why the name change? New studies showed that *not everyone* with NVLD has every difficulty. The one thing they all have in common is a visual-spatial deficit. The researchers suggested that this should be the only required feature for diagnosis. Everything else, the executive function, social skills, motor coordination and everything else I experienced might be part of the picture, but not always.

That made me feel a bit upset, because I *do* have all those other challenges. It felt like they were saying, "Only this part of your brain matters." If DVSD becomes the new diagnosis, I might need to get extra labels just to explain all the other things I deal with. That feels unfair. It's likely I might end up with three diagnoses instead of one which encompasses everything - instead of just being understood as a whole person.

Where We Are Now, and Why It Matters

The NVLD Project's research has shown that around 4% of children may have NVLD (Margolis et al., 2020). That means millions of people around the world are living with it, even if they don't know it. That makes me feel less alone.

There are still challenges. NVLD (or DVSD) isn't in the DSM yet. That means some kids won't be diagnosed, and schools won't be funded to offer support and the early intervention which is so important.

Things are changing. Researchers are now working on consensus criteria for DVSD, using brain imaging, long-term studies, and clinical experiences to shape the way forward. The updated proposal is expected to be published soon in the *Journal of the American Academy of Child & Adolescent Psychiatry*.

For me, no matter what they call it, NVLD or DVSD, I know it's real. I know what it feels like to live with it. And I know that understanding my brain has made me stronger, more confident, and more able to help others too.

15

NVLD: What it Feels Like

It's hard to explain what it feels like to have NVLD. Honestly, most of the time, I don't know exactly how I am different from everyone else. I just know that I am. It's like I am on this strange journey that no one else is on, and I don't have a map. I feel like I am constantly guessing how to do things that other people already understand, and even when I try really hard, I still mess it up and don't know why.

Social communication is one of the hardest things. It's not that I don't want to talk to people: I do, but I overthink everything. Every single sentence I say has already been through this massive filter in my brain. I'm always scared I'll say the wrong thing. My biggest fear is someone looking me straight in the eye and saying, "That wasn't appropriate for you to say." So I try to think everything through. And if I don't know if it's okay to say something, I just don't say it. It makes me feel exhausted all the time.

After conversations, I worry for ages. I worry that someone's going to call Mum and complain about something I said or didn't say.

Even with my sister, I get scared she'll message Mum and say, "She was so bad at social stuff today." It feels like I'm under scrutiny all the time, even though I'm not. Sometimes I set myself challenges not to speak, thinking, "Nobody wants to hear from you anyway. Just be quiet. Be invisible." I've told myself to be non-verbal for hours at social events. It doesn't usually last, because I love to network and joke around.

I constantly apologise. I apologise when I don't even know what I've done wrong. I say sorry if I think I might have upset someone or made a mistake, even with small things like schoolwork. I say sorry if I'm not sure whether I've done the right thing. Mum is always saying, "Stop apologising. You haven't done anything wrong. You just made a mistake." But it's not that simple for me. It's really hard to know the difference between doing something wrong and just doing my work wrongly, or saying something wrong. What's the line between making a mistake and saying something inappropriate that crosses a boundary? When I told the boys at school that I wore nappies, I didn't realise that was sharing private information. I didn't know it was inappropriate. I felt terrible and didn't even know how to fix it. I still carry that kind of thing, memories of my past mistakes. Sometimes I wonder if I'm really saying sorry for just existing, sorry for being me, sorry for making things harder for people, sorry for making their lives more miserable. It all comes back to feeling like a burden.

I sometimes start things with, "This is probably a weird question…" just in case I've already done something wrong without knowing. When I'm laughing with others, sometimes I don't even know what the joke is. I just laugh along so I don't feel left out. I want to be part of the group too, but I'm scared of being embarrassed or humiliated. I laughed because everyone else did, not because I got the joke.

There are times when I don't know what to say and panic. Once, when someone said they were pregnant, but they were joking about other things too, I wasn't sure if it was real or sarcastic. Everyone else said, "Congratulations," but I didn't want to embarrass myself. What if they weren't actually pregnant and I took it seriously? That would have been worse. So I just said nothing and then overthought that too.

I also have really strong visual–spatial challenges. I get lost even in places I've been many times. One time we were nearly home, and I suddenly said, "Are we near that Vegan Yum place?" Mum said, "No ... that's on the other side of Brisbane." It was actually over an hour away. I had no idea where we were, even though we were almost at our house. I think I just got totally turned around in my head. It's a weird feeling, never knowing where you are in the world.

Another time I was out on my bike, and I thought I was taking the long way home, but it just kept getting longer and longer. I had fun at first, thinking I knew where I was going. Then I was thinking, "Where am I?" I ended up at a church in the opposite direction and still thought I could get home by riding just a bit further. I honestly didn't know how far away I had gone. I planned in my head where I'd sleep if I got stuck. "Could I sleep in a bush? What if my phone is dead or has no signal? What if no one is around?" That's just what I think about.

Recognising familiar places can be tricky. One time I turned around at the neighbour's door and didn't realise our house was right across the street. Another time, Mum dropped me off at our next door neighbour's house and I freaked out. I screamed, "Don't leave me! How am I going to get home from here?" Mum was literally just driving around the corner. I was only two houses away from home but I didn't recognise it. I was terrified. Mum patiently explained that all I had to do was watch her turn the corner and follow her car. I did. I was okay. That was probably an important step in me starting to develop some independence and learn my way around my neighbourhood.

In shopping centres, if I come out of the toilets, I might not know which way to go. There was this time when I went into the toilets near Smiggle, and Mum even pointed out Smiggle as a landmark. But when I came out, I turned the wrong way, confidently walked out the opposite end of the alley, and just kept going. I didn't even notice Smiggle wasn't there. I was just striding confidently into the centre. I thought I looked really independent, but I was actually going the wrong way. Mum asked where I was going. "I'm looking for Smiggle," I replied, totally unaware that the alley had led to a completely different part of the shopping centre.

At school, every new year, I had to relearn how to get from the car to my classroom. If the classroom changed, I was lost. I'd go to the tuckshop just because it was familiar and then figure out how to get to the uniform shop from there, even if the uniform shop was closer to where I started. I just couldn't recognise which building was which because they all looked the same. Once, I confidently walked into the wrong year's classroom and tried to act cool like I was supposed to be there, but I definitely wasn't. IT was my old classroom. My brain had remembered the rote pathway to last year's classroom.

Maths is another thing that's hard. People always say, "Imagine a number line," or "Picture this in your head," but I can't. I can't visualise things like that. I can see words in my head really clearly so spelling is fine because I can picture the word. But numbers are just symbols to me. I've actually wished that numbers had capital and lowercase versions like letters, so I could treat them like spelling. It would help me learn them better. For me, two isn't just "2." I have to think, "Okay, it means one and one."

Crossing roads is really stressful. Sometimes I can't work out which way the cars are coming from, especially with multiple lanes or slip lanes. If there's no car, I can't tell which direction the lane is supposed to go. And car parks are horrible. Everything echoes and I can't hear where the cars are. I judge if a car is moving by whether its lights are on. If the lights are off, I assume it's parked, even if it's not. One time I was nearly hit by an electric car and only noticed because the brakes squealed. That startled me. I didn't see or hear it coming at all.

Knowing where my own body is can be hard. I bump my head or my hip all the time. I misjudge where things are. I'll go to pick up a guinea pig and forget to check where their paws are. I've hit my head putting away dishes, knocked cupboard doors, walked into walls and other people. One time Mum said, "Duck your head!" at the playground, but I thought I was clear because my eyes were under the bar. I forgot to leave room for the top of my head. These things happen all the time.

Sport is tricky too. I once got hit in the face by a drone in Year 2 because I didn't realise it was that close. I tried to move but misjudged how fast or far I needed to go. I ask people how they avoid getting hit by balls and they say, "You just look where the ball is."

But for me, that's not enough. The ball moves! I've walked the long way around people just to avoid getting hit. I look weird, but I'd rather look weird than get hit.

Being a sports trainer has helped me a little. It has taught me to look around and be more aware. It has helped me feel like I'm not just weird or "special needs." I feel like a human. I feel useful. People in sport are often more relaxed. If you get something wrong, they say, "It's fine." That has helped me give myself more grace. I wanted to be a sports trainer because I want to be the calm one—the one who helps, not the one falling apart. I want to change healthcare by being that steady person for someone else.

I still worry that I stand out, that people don't really want me there, or that they are only including me to be polite. But I am learning that it's okay to be me. I'm not some mistake. I'm not just a problem. I'm trying, and I have value, even if I sometimes forget where I am or walk into doors or get scared crossing the street.

Key Takeaways:

Be patient with kids who get lost easily. If a child struggles with directions, don't get frustrated. Use simple landmarks and teach one step at a time. Help them build confidence slowly and celebrate little wins along the way.

Understand that overthinking is real. Telling a child to "just relax" doesn't work when their brain is stuck on what went wrong. Instead, point out what went well. That helps rebuild confidence and reduce the self-doubt they carry.

Don't say "just visualise". If a child struggles with visual thinking, they need clear steps, not vague ideas. Use verbal cues, demonstrations, actual hands-on materials and repetition to help them understand as they cannot 'visualise' things in their mind. This applies to all subject areas. They cannot visualise a number chart or action in a story.

Let kids practise social interactions without pressure. Talking to people can feel overwhelming. Practise what to say, give examples, and remind them it's okay to mess up. Social skills are learned skills, not automatic.

If they laugh at the wrong time or miss the joke, don't shame them. Social cues can be confusing. Gently explain what happened and reassure them it's okay not to get it right all the time. Watch videos and rewind them to analyse and explain social cues.

Recognise how tiring it is to filter every thought. Kids who constantly double-check what they are hearing or saying might seem quiet or anxious. Give them space to rest. That kind of mental effort is exhausting and sometimes they just need to be away from people for a while. Provide a safe space where they can retreat when needed.

Help them find roles where they feel included. Being a class helper can give a child a sense of belonging. Find ways for them to contribute that match their strengths. They might be great at helping a friend with reading, but kids with NVLD are not going to be good messengers because they will just get lost, unless they go with a buddy.

Don't rely on "common sense". Explain things clearly. What feels obvious to others might not make sense to a neurodivergent child, especially if they interpret everything literally. Break things down and be ready to repeat things more than once and in different ways.

Create safe spaces where mistakes aren't a big deal. When kids feel safe to make mistakes without being teased or punished, they are more likely to try. Show them that learning is a process, not something you have to get right the first time.

Let them know you see their effort. Just getting through the day can take a lot. Tell them, "I know that was hard, and I'm proud of you." Those words can make a huge difference.

Reassure kids who apologise often. If a child keeps saying sorry, it might be because they feel like a burden. Gently let them know they are not. Remind them they are loved, wanted, and valued just as they are.

16

Social Communication: Misunderstanding People

Social communication has never been easy for me. People think that just because I can talk, I must be good at communicating, but it's not that simple. Social communication is about more than using words. It's about understanding how and when to use them, what people mean when they speak, how body language fits in, and what's expected in different situations.

I overthink almost every conversation. Before I speak, my brain goes through all the different things that could go wrong. I worry constantly that I'll say the wrong thing, sound rude, or embarrass myself. After conversations, I go over every word again in my head. I worry that someone might call my mum and tell her all the things I did wrong. I wonder, "Was that okay? Did I talk too much? Was that weird?" The hard part is that I never really know. My biggest fear is someone turning to me and saying, "That was not appropriate." I try so hard to avoid that. It makes me second-guess everything. That's why sometimes, I just stay quiet. I think if I don't speak, I can't say the wrong thing, but sometimes, that silence can feel really lonely.

Even when I try to join in, it can be hard, especially when people tell jokes or use sarcasm. I often don't understand what they really mean. I might laugh along so I don't seem left out, but inside, I feel confused and anxious. There have been so many times I've asked, "Was that a joke?" or "Are they serious?" and the answer isn't always clear. One time, someone said they were pregnant, and everyone said "Congratulations" in a voice that sounded sarcastic. I didn't know if it was a joke or not, so I said nothing, and then worried that I had offended them.

Sometimes I say things that are true for me, but they come out in a way that upsets others. When I said I hadn't had any friends, I didn't mean to hurt anyone. I was just being honest. However, I have learnt that honesty isn't always seen as kind. That has been really hard for me. I want to be truthful, but I also don't want to get into trouble.

When I was little, I didn't really understand who I should talk to or what I should share. I once told some Year 3 boys that I wore nappies. I thought if they knew, they'd understand and be kind. Instead, I was mocked, teased and bullied. I didn't understand what was happening. I couldn't understand why they were laughing. That's when I started to learn that being open can be dangerous., and that made me even more anxious about social situations.

At school, I got into trouble for things I didn't understand. A teacher told us all to stop talking in the line. I didn't talk at all. I stayed completely silent, but I made a small gesture to my friend to come and be my partner. The teacher told me off. "I said no talking!" I was so confused. I hadn't broken the rule. I had not spoken even one word, but I still got into trouble. That's what happens when people expect you to "just know" what they mean without saying it clearly. It made me scared of making mistakes when I thought I was doing the right thing. I lived in fear of being in trouble, or being sent to the office.

Sometimes I feel like a victim in conversations. I'm trying so hard to understand what people mean and keep up, but I'm always one step behind. When I told a teacher aide I wanted to run away, I didn't mean I was going to. I was just letting her know I felt overwhelmed. She took it really seriously and told the head of the school. I was suspended and threatened with expulsion. I wasn't trying to cause trouble, but I ended up feeling like I was being punished for saying how I felt. I thought it must be safer to keep everything inside, to be quiet.

There are moments where I'm not sure if people mean what they say. If someone says "I'm proud of you," I wonder, "Are they really? Or are they just saying that to be nice?" I doubt compliments because I've spent so long being unsure if I'm doing things right. It's not that I don't want to believe people, it's just that I find it hard to trust what I can't clearly see or understand. If I say something funny and people laugh, I freeze. Was it a good laugh or a mean one? Did I say something silly without realising it? Did I accidentally offend someone? I want so badly to connect, but every part of my brain is working overtime trying to figure out what's really going on. What do they really mean?

There is also the way people use their bodies and faces to communicate. That part is really confusing for me. I can tell when someone is happy or sad if it's really obvious, but subtle things go right over my head. If someone is smiling with a hint of sarcasm, or if they say something serious with a funny tone, I won't always know how to react. That makes group conversations hard. I feel like I'm watching a play in another language, where everyone else knows the script, but I'm making it up as I go. All of this makes social communication feel like a performance. One where I'm scared to mess up, even when I'm trying my best. I don't want to feel like I'm being judged all the time. I just want to connect with people in a way that feels safe and kind and clear.

Because it is so exhausting, sometimes I just need to retreat from the world. I hide out in the toilet or stay in my room with the door shut, just to get a break from all the thinking and pressure. Other times, I go for a bike ride or take my guinea pigs to the park. Being outside, away from people, gives me space to breathe. It helps me calm my mind and feel like myself again. I need those quiet moments to reset, so I can keep facing a world that doesn't always make sense to me.

I'm also learning how to advocate for myself. I've started telling Mum when I'm overwhelmed and need a break. I'm learning that it's okay to ask for time alone, and that listening to my own needs isn't selfish. It's actually really important. I might not always have the words to explain everything, but I'm getting better at saying, "I need some space," or "I just need a bit of quiet right now." That's a big step forward for me.

Key Takeaways:

Social communication is more than just talking. It's not just about words. You also need to understand all the nonverbal cues, the tone of voice, facial expressions, rolling eyes, body language, timing, and unwritten social rules. These are the areas I struggle with, and I know many other neurodivergent kids struggle with these too.

Teach facial expressions in context. Be aware that we may miss or totally misinterpret things, like when I thought Grandma was angry, but she was concentrating on her puzzle. That's why her eyebrows were down in the middle. When kids learn about facial expressions, let them know the same facial expression, mouth position, eyebrow angle, can mean different things depending on the social context.

Be aware of our literal interpretations. Some kids sound confident when they talk, but that doesn't mean they understand what's happening socially. Kids who interpret things literally may be totally misunderstanding a conversation, especially if someone is being sarcastic. Help us interpret what is happening and check that we understand what is going on, what we are required to do or how we should respond in certain situations.

Reassure us after social situations. If we look anxious or unsure, tell us something we did well or help explain what happened. A little reassurance can stop us from replaying the moment over and over, trying to work out what we did wrong.

Avoid vague feedback like "That wasn't appropriate." Those kinds of comments are confusing. Instead, explain what didn't work, why it didn't, and what we could try next time. Be gentle and remember, we're learning.

Teach social rules without using shame or punishment. Go through examples together. Talk about real situations. Draw little social story cartoons. Let us practise in role play situations with safe adults before we need to try with kids and allow us to make mistakes without feeling like we've failed.

Be open and honest with the class. Talk about the way we struggle with social cues and encourage the class to help us and protect us on the playground. Don't allow bullying or teasing. When people are informed and aware, it increases tolerance and acceptance and reduces the risks of being targeted. Bringing things out into the open educates everyone to help create kindness in the community.

Let us ask about jokes, sarcasm, or tone without embarrassment. If we don't get something, help us understand without teasing or rolling your eyes. Answer with kindness. Curiosity is how we learn.

Recognise how much effort it takes to fit in. Trying to get it right all the time is exhausting. Every spoken word, every reaction, analysing every facial expression, voice volume and tone takes energy as we wonder if we 'got it right'. Please allow us time to withdraw from the demands of social situations sometimes too.

Going to the library or bathroom, retreating into a little tent or cubby, or even device time can be a relief for us from the pressures of trying to communicate.

Encourage honesty but teach us who we can talk to about certain things, and how to say things safely. We might be very direct or blunt or hurtful. We might share too much with strangers. Help us find respectful ways to share our thoughts and protect ourselves from ridicule.

Believe us when we say we're trying. Even when it doesn't look like it, we're working hard to understand and connect. Your support, patience, and understanding mean everything.

Make communication feel safe, even when we mess up. If we say the wrong thing or get confused, don't shame us. Nobody is perfect. Stay calm, stay kind, and let us try again. That's how we can learn to trust.

17

Executive Function: Not Getting it Right

In the early years of school, things were okay. Teachers usually provide a lot of support to young children. However, by Year 4, things started to fall apart. That's when teachers began expecting much more independence. That was hard for me.

We all started learning a musical instrument. My music day just happened to be the same day as PE. Because we weren't allowed to wear our sports uniform to and from school, I had to bring an extra bag with my PE clothes, sports shoes, and hat, or sometimes togs, towel, sun shirt, and thongs. On top of that, I had to carry my clarinet. It was a lot.

Mum tried really hard to help me. She made laminated checklists for each day of the week so I could tick off what I needed as I packed my bag, but I would often forget to tick things off and think I had already packed them. There were so many days when Mum would get a phone call at work asking her to bring in my school shirt, or pants, or hat. It happened so often that she left a spare uniform at the school office just to save time and get me back to class more quickly. Some people thought I was doing it on purpose to avoid maths, but I wasn't. I was overwhelmed.

Packing my school bag was another major issue. I couldn't seem to do it during the day. Teachers would see my lunchbox in one place, my bag in another, and my hat somewhere else—all within about a two-metre radius. My belongings were often confiscated to try to "teach me a lesson" about looking after my things, but it didn't work. It just me feel more inadequate. How come other kids could look after their things, but mine seemed to be scattered everywhere?

In Year 5, things became even harder when we started moving around the school for different subjects. I not only had to pack the right equipment for that day, but I also had to plan ahead after each break. One way Mum tried to help was by buying separate laptop bags for every subject. Everything I needed for that lesson was kept in the one bag, so I only had to pick up the two bags I needed for that session. That definitely helped. One afternoon a week, I had PE followed by technology. That meant I had to change into my PE clothes at lunchtime, remember to take my hat and water bottle, and also take my computer with me. One day I remembered my hat and water bottle but forgot my computer. By the time I walked back from PE to the classroom to collect my computer and then tried to find my way to the technology room (which was not easy with my visual–spatial challenges), I was 20 minutes late for class. Of course, I got into trouble. Another time, Mum wrote a reminder note and put it on my lunchbox to help me remember the computer. When I got in the car, she asked if it worked. I proudly said, "Yes! I remembered the computer!" However, I had forgotten my water bottle so I wasn't allowed to play sport that day.

It was always something. No matter how hard I tried, I was always forgetting something or getting into trouble. It wore me down. The stress and the feeling that I was always doing something wrong added to my anxiety and depression. Eventually, Mum said she would homeschool me. That was the best decision ever.

Even now, my lack of organisational skills still impacts my work. I used to struggle with how to lay things out on a page. I didn't know how to complete an assignment unless it was broken down step-by-step. In the extension class, teachers assumed I didn't need help. They expected me to do a PowerPoint presentation about endangered animals. I didn't know how to start, so I spent all my time designing a fancy title slide. I didn't even get to the research. Teachers should never assume a certain level of capability based on age or what class a student is in. Just because I was in the extension group didn't mean I didn't need support. I needed the right accommodations to show what I was really capable of.

Being homeschooled made a huge difference. Mum taught me how to break tasks down into introduction, body, and conclusion. She helped me learn to sort relevant from irrelevant information—another area NVLD kids struggle with. Once I knew what steps to take, I could do the work. Now I plan things automatically, which has helped me write articles and give presentations.

NVLD affects more than learning. It affects every aspect of life at home, at school, at play and in the wider community. It impacts friendships, emotional wellbeing, organisation, independence, academic achievements and even physical safety. It is not something we will ever grow out of, but with the right supports, we can learn to be happy with who we are and thrive.

Key Takeaways:

Don't assume we're coping just because we speak well or are in the extension class. Strong verbal skills or being in an extension group doesn't mean we don't need help. We might still struggle with organisation, executive functioning, and emotional regulation. Always look at the full picture.

Always look beyond the behaviour. Ask why we might be struggling. If we forget our gear or don't finish a task, it's probably not because we're lazy or avoiding the learning. It may be because something wasn't working for us. We may not have fully understood the instruction. We may be having difficulty making a plan, working out where to start or what to do next.

Support our executive functioning with clear, step-by-step instructions. We can do the task, but only if we understand the steps. Don't assume we "should know" what to do just because of our age or ability in other areas. Break things down clearly and give examples. Planning templates can be really helpful for us, especially if we can apply the same template to multiple subjects and tasks. Keep checking we know the next step in the process.

Give us tools and strategies that really work. Checklists, subject bags with everything we need in one bag, and labelled folders can make a big difference. They need to be simple and easy to use consistently. Show us how to use them and check in with us regularly to see if we need additional supports.

Understand that repetition is important for us. People with NVLD learn by rote. We might need to be reminded more than once. That doesn't mean we're not trying. It just means our brain needs help holding onto all the steps. The more we can repeat the steps and apply them across multiple areas of our lives, the easier things become for us.

Kids with neurodiversity and executive function difficulties require help long past the usual age. I still need help with organisation and planning. I didn't reach Year 4 or 5 and suddenly not need help any more. I will probably need support for many years. Be guided by the child's abilities not the same chronological age expectations used for neurotypical children.

Don't punish us for being disorganised. Taking away our belongings or giving detentions won't teach us anything except that we're always getting it wrong. We need support, not shame. Help us to put the things in our bags, or clean our rooms step by step. Seeing a big mess can be too overwhelming and we don't know where to start. Having someone guide us with suggestions like, "How about you put your lunchbox in first" or "Start by collecting all the books or shoes" can make a big difference to help us get started, or help us maintain focus through to completion.

Plan effective visual materials. Busy worksheets and lots of visual cues can actually make things harder for us. Plain written instructions are easier to follow. Make sure worksheets or workbooks follow logical sequence down the page without multiple insets or different sections and columns. Make sure PowerPoint slides are also in logical sequence, not cluttered or visually overwhelming. Increasing line spacing can help too as it increases the amount of white space on the page and feels less overwhelming. We sometimes need books enlarged. Having books that allow plenty of space for responses directly under the question are great because we have difficulty finding where we are up to when we have to look from one book to another.

Be direct—don't expect us to pick up on hints or sarcasm. We often miss implied, sarcastic meanings like, "I love the way you packed your bag." Say exactly what you mean in a kind, clear way. We're not trying to be difficult. We're trying to understand.

Don't expect "common sense". Express things clearly and explicitly. What seems obvious to other kids might be confusing for us. Give us the same considerations you would give a younger student learning something for the first time, even when we reach high school. We don't always generalise from one situation to another. Packing my school bag is different from packing my swimming bag. Writing a plan for an essay in English won't be carried across to writing a plan for an essay in History unless you tell us it is the same and explain that we can use the same structure..

Recognise that being forgetful can add to our anxiety. When we keep forgetting things, it doesn't just affect our grades, it affects how we feel about ourselves. A constant stream of "What? You forgot again!" can lead to loss of self-esteem and depression. That's why Mum put a spare uniform in the office for me during swimming term. She understood it was causing me stress if I forgot something and it was affecting how I felt about myself.

Help us feel successful by showing us how to plan. Don't do the work for us, but teach us how to sort out relevant and irrelevant information, break down assignments, and start tasks step-by-step. With the right planning help, we can do amazing things.

Acknowledge our effort, even when the outcome isn't perfect. If we made it to class with the right gear, finished part of a task, or even remembered one thing from a long list, notice it. Let us know you see us trying.

Make school feel like a place where we can grow, not just survive. Create an environment where it's safe to ask for help, where mistakes aren't punished, and where we're supported to do things in a way that works for our brain.

18

Visual-Spatial: Where in the World is Siobhan?!

Even from a young age, Mum began noticing that I had a lot of trouble understanding the visual world around me. One of the earliest signs was that I couldn't figure out how to stand up in shallow water. I couldn't work out how to use a basic stacking ring toy. She would bring it out every six months to try again, but even by the time I was four or five, I still couldn't do it. Jigsaw puzzles were another struggle. I didn't understand what an "edge" or a "corner" piece was. To me, lots of pieces had straight bits. When I was about three, it took me six months to master a simple three-piece puzzle, and that only happened because I spent hours pulling it apart and putting it back together again. Rote learning was a strength for me, but figuring things out visually was not.

At the same time, I was writing full stories at kindy. Words and letters were easy. I loved reading and writing and would spend ages playing hospitals and making charts for my "patients." That contrast—great with words but struggling with visual–spatial tasks—was a big clue. When I saw the OT, she tested my spatial copying skills. I could copy a straight line, but as soon as it became an upside-down "L" shape, I struggled. As the tasks became more complex, it became clear that I had real deficits in visual–spatial perception. How could it be that I could write complex letter shapes, but could not even copy a simple two line design?

Another thing Mum noticed was how I focused on tiny details in pictures but missed the big picture. Once I was playing a 'spot the difference' game on the iPad. It was Easter, and the image showed a woven basket of eggs. One of the differences was a missing piece of the weaving. I looked up and told Mum, "The brick is missing." She had no idea what I meant. She looked around the house thinking a brick had fallen out of the wall. When I pointed at the screen, she realised I was talking about the basket. It was a piece of the basket missing, not a brick! She couldn't understand how I could look at the basket and think it was a brick in a wall. I had completely missed the big picture.

My speech therapist once asked me to describe a picture. There was a campfire with sparks, but I thought they were fireworks. I just couldn't interpret what I was seeing. Pictures often confused me. In one story called *I Want Some Honey*, a seal wants to try honey for the first time. Because he said "I want" and not "Can I please have some?", and because the picture showed him with his mouth open and teeth showing, I thought he was angry. I shouted, "I WANT SOME HONEY!" in an angry voice. Mum asked why I thought he was mad. When she covered the picture and read just the words, I realised he wasn't angry. He was actually sad because he felt he was missing out, never having tasted honey. It was strange for a young child to comprehend the meaning of a text better without the pictures. Most kids use the picture clues to help them read.

Maths was especially hard. I didn't understand symmetry properly until about Year 6 or 7 during homeschooling. Place value and fractions were confusing. Geometry? Forget it. Rotations, translations—especially the questions that said, "Look at this shape. Imagine it has been rotated 270 degrees. Which of these is the result: A, B, C, or D?" I had no hope. And number lines? I could never estimate where halfway was, let alone one-eighth. Scale was extremely challenging. The same amount of space between the lines might mean 10mL on one jug and 100mL on a different jug. How are you supposed to make sense of that?

Numbers didn't make sense to me the way they do for other people. I couldn't "see" a number in my head the way I could see a letter. I had to learn what "two" meant like it was a word definition—one thing and another thing. That's two. I couldn't visualise it naturally. I always wished there was a capital one and a lowercase one, like letters, so it felt more real.

My handwriting was affected. Trying to form letters neatly inside the blue and red lines was incredibly frustrating. The lines kept changing. One year, they were only widely spaced blue lines. The next year, there were red and blue with a dotted blue line, then no dotted blue line, then only blue but close together. Each year, I had to learn a whole new way to write my letters. It took so much effort, I would forget to focus on what I was actually writing. I worked much better on blank paper.

Safety was a big issue too, and still is. I can't estimate distances properly. I've misjudged where my head is when climbing into bed, ducking under bars at the playground, or putting things into cupboards. I've bumped my head so many times just because I didn't leave enough space for the top of my head. I can't just "know" where my body ends. I have to learn it. I also walk into things like door frames and walls. Sometimes I even knock my hip into the edge of a bench or bang into cupboard corners because I thought I had more room.

Crossing roads is terrifying. I struggle to work out which way cars are coming. Especially when there are multiple lanes or slip lanes. It's hard to figure out who's turning, where they're going, or how fast. Electric cars make it worse. They're silent. I once crossed the road and didn't even realise a car was coming until it slammed on its brakes. I still flash back to that moment. I also get confused about whether something is a driveway or a footpath. Carparks are just noise and shapes. The only way I know a car is moving is if the lights are on.

I've also had trouble finding my way around places. Shopping centres are especially confusing. Everything looks the same. Once, Mum told me to look for Smiggle on my way out of the toilets. I turned the wrong way and confidently walked into a completely different part of the centre. Another time, when we were moving house, I turned around at the neighbour's front door and couldn't even recognise our own house across the street.

School buildings were the worst. They all looked alike. When I went into Year 4, I couldn't remember how to get to the toilets from my new classroom, so I went back to the Year 3 block and walked in like nothing had changed. I had to learn the way from the car to my classroom every single year. If I was going to the uniform shop, I had to walk past the tuckshop because that's the only way I remembered how to get there, even though the uniform shop was actually closer.

Visual-Spatial Problem Solving – A Daily Struggle That No One Sees

Visual-spatial problem solving affects almost every single thing I do, even if no one else sees it. It's not just about schoolwork or puzzles. It's the reason why some things that seem really easy for other kids are actually super hard for me. Things like getting dressed, finding my way around, folding clothes, using a zipper, or even hanging up a jumper. It affects my independence, my confidence, and how other people treat me. Most of all, it affects how I see myself.

When I was little, getting dressed was already a challenge. Underwear has three holes, and when you're small, it's not that easy to tell which one is the waist and which are the leg holes. Then you have to figure out which side is the front and which is the back. Doing up buttons is tricky, but press studs are almost impossible. You can't even see the two bits that are supposed to click together, so I often just avoid clothes with press studs altogether. Zippers that you have to line up before they'll zip, like those on jackets, are really hard too. If I do wear those, I usually need Mum to help me. I've learned to avoid buying them when I can.

Finding the armholes in a jumper can be confusing. When I try to hang something up, it's a disaster. Jumpers seem to have holes everywhere—the sleeves, the bottom, the neck—and if there's a hood, it's even worse. I sometimes have to lay the jumper flat on my bed and figure out what's what before I can even attempt to put it on a coat hanger. Other times, I just guess. I shove the hanger through some hole and hope for the best. Not surprisingly, there's usually a pile of clothes on the floor of my cupboard because I can't hang them up properly, or they fall off into my shoe box and get tangled. Then Mum is certainly not too happy when they end up back in the washing!

Folding clothes isn't easy either. My method usually ends up being more of a roll than a fold. And drawers? Total chaos. Even when I neatly stack piles of shirts, undies and shorts, they all end up tangled into one big mess because I have to rummage around to find anything. It got too frustrating. So Mum bought me some shelves and big boxes instead. We labelled each one clearly—shorts, undies, shirts—and now I can find what I need much more easily. It still takes work, but at least I don't get overwhelmed just trying to get dressed.

Something as simple as ruling a straight line in a notebook can be stressful. I remember trying to rule a line and couldn't work out why the ruler wouldn't sit properly. It turned out that it was getting caught on the spiral edge of the notebook, but I hadn't used that type of book before, so I didn't know. Mum moved it across and it worked—but by then, I already felt like I'd failed.

Going places on my own has always been a challenge. One time, Mum let me ride my bike to the local shops. I made it there just fine. I felt so proud of myself. However, on the way back, I got completely lost. I didn't realise I had taken a wrong turn until I ended up near a church. I used the church as a landmark to get home, but I was gone for hours. I worried that because I had failed in my mind, Mum wouldn't let me go out alone any more. I used to think through backup plans just in case I got lost. "Where would I sleep if I couldn't get home?" I'd picture sleeping in a bush or near a church because I didn't trust that I'd be able to find my way back. It was scary, even if I pretended it was fun.

As a sports trainer, visual-spatial problems follow me. I have to judge where the ball is and whether it's safe to run onto the field. Sometimes I get it wrong. I've almost been hit by balls that I didn't realise were close. People say, "Just look where the ball is," but the ball moves so quickly and I can't always predict where it's going, so I take the long way around and try to avoid the chaos. That job has helped me learn to be more aware of my surroundings. It has taught me that I don't always have to be perfect, and that I'm not weird—I'm just learning differently.

Key Takeaways

Use clear, language-based directions with familiar landmarks. Instead of saying, "Go over there," try "Walk past the red bin and turn left at the big tree." Visual–spatial instructions can be confusing. Words help more.

Don't assume we know how to estimate space. If we need to duck under something, for example, explain exactly how. "Bend your knees more or your head won't fit". Don't be upset if we make errors in judgement like banging into people or knocking into things because we thought we would fit in that space. I lost count of the number of times I banged the wall because I was so sure I could do a cartwheel between my bed and the wall in the 1m space.

Remember team sports are difficult, especially ball games. Games like netball or soccer are difficult as we cannot predict where the ball will go after it has been thrown or kicked. Take care we are not vulnerable during these activities as other kids can be cruel to kids less able. Maybe allocate teams rather than leaving kids to choose their own team members as we will always be left until last or never be chosen.

Give us repetition and routines to build visual memory. We need lots of practice walking the same path or doing the same task to remember it visually. Routines aren't boring for us. They are crucial for our safety.

Provide safe chances to practise independence with support. Let the child try things like packing their bag but stay close in case they get stuck or frustrated when it doesn't work. Don't do it for them, but assist with hints like, "Maybe try putting your lunchbox in the other way, with the handle facing the front of the bag." Independence builds confidence when they experience success.

Help us organise our clothes and label them clearly. Drawers are very confusing if they contain different items of clothing. Once we rummage for a particular favourite shirt, all the piles become a big mess, and we can't find anything. Boxes work better than drawers. Use words or coloured labels. Label the boxes with words and pictures if necessary and keep things in the same place. This helps us find what we need without panic. Don't get upset if the box gets a bit messy either. If we can find our clothes, it's okay.

Allocate the child a special place for their belongings, preferably at the end of a shelf. At school, I could never find my clarinet among the other instruments in the classroom. The teacher made a little space at the end of one shelf where mine could be placed and let everyone else know only mine went there. That was very helpful. It relieved a lot of stress.

Let us go at our own pace with everyday tasks. Rushing makes it worse. We might need more time to get dressed, pack up, or follow instructions. Shaming us or trying to make us go faster only adds pressure. Give us space. Getting up half an hour earlier is a better option. When we get stressed, our amygdala fires off and we can't think clearly.

Encourage our strengths. We might be great at writing, helping younger kids, telling funny stories or solving problems with words. Higher order thinking skills like creating, or evaluating can be our strengths if we use our language. Celebrate those things. They remind us that we're more than our struggles.

Remember that mathematics involving visual-spatial perception will be very challenging. Symmetry, fractions, graphs, maps, geometry, place value all require visual perception. We cannot visualise things in our minds so if you ask us how many faces or edges a shape has, we will need to hold it to count them. We really struggle with online maths as we can't physically manipulate the objects. We may need to copy the shape and cut it out before we can rotate it or fold it. Sometimes we may need help to draw a diagram in order to understand the task. With the right scaffolding, we can learn.

Visual interpretation can also be affected. Help us understand visual cues for pictures in books, advertisements and cartoons and make sure we are interpreting them correctly. Make sure we understand the picture in its entirety, that we haven't only seen one detail. For example, just because the picture of the dog shows its teeth doesn't mean it is angry and growling. It might be panting because it is hot. Remember, visual clues are nonverbal clues.

Develop strategies to help us keep our place when reading. Putting paper or a ruler over the line we just read or encouraging us to keep our finger on the side of the row we are reading helps us if we are distracted. Without it, we have no idea which side of the book we were reading or where we were on the page so we need to start back at the top of the left side all over again.

Minimise copying from one location to another. Copying from the board, a computer screen or another book is so hard. We need to look up and find where we are up to, then we have to look back at the book we are writing in to find the spot where we were working. When we look up again, we have to start back at the top before we can find the next part. Providing worksheets where we can read and complete the task directly below the question are best. If we need to learn scientific diagrams, print them out for us or model drawing them for us slowly, step by step, helping us position them correctly on the page.

Trying to write inside the lines can drain our concentration. If you want to know what we understand or what we can create, give us blank paper so we don't have to stress about writing in the lines and we can focus on the content. Be aware that changing lines from year to year can be very confusing. Red and blue lines, dotted lines, no red lines … so stressful! It's like learning to form letters all over again each year.

Be our protector in risky places. Water, roads and car parks are all dangerous places for kids with visual-spatial deficits. Even if we seem old enough to cross the road alone, we might misjudge distance or speed. Stay nearby. Don't take chances with our safety. We will need your support long past the usual age of independence.

Celebrate the small wins—we worked hard for them. Getting to school with all our gear, remembering to pack something, or finishing a small task might seem tiny to others, but for us, they're huge. Let us be proud. Celebrate our little achievements.

Our lives are tough, so boost our self-esteem whenever you can. We need it.

19

Sensory Processing: When It's All Too Much

My body doesn't always do what I want it to do. That's because my sensory processing is different. Sometimes I feel too much. Other times, I don't feel enough. It's like my senses are turned up too high or too low, and I can't always predict how they'll react. It can be really confusing and exhausting. Having a severe visual-spatial deficit doesn't help either.

One of the hardest things is proprioception, which is my sense of body awareness. I don't always know where my body is in space. I bump into things and people, misjudge distances, and walk into door frames and bench corners - THAT hurts! When I try to duck under something, I only look with my eyes, so if my eyes are below the bar, I think I'm fine. Then I hit my head because I didn't leave room for the top of my head. That's something most people don't even think about, but I have to. I'm better now, but that is because I learnt through pain.

When I'm putting a glass away in the cupboard or loading the dishwasher, I have to plan every movement carefully. Where is the cupboard? Where is my head? Will I scrape my leg on the cupboard or dishwasher? These are tiny everyday actions that other people just do with little to no thought. However, for me, I have had to learn every step through trial and error ... and sometimes getting it wrong.

Touch is also tricky. I can't always feel how much pressure I'm using when I pat my guinea pigs, so I have to be as gentle as I can. When I'm picking them up, I have to remind myself to be careful not to place their feet in the wrong spot so their toes don't get caught in the cage. It makes me scared I'll hurt them because of my lack of awareness even though I'm trying so hard to be gentle.

Walking can be hard. When I was young, Mum would have to hold my hand walking along footpaths as I constantly tripped on uneven pavements. One time, as a teenager, I tripped and fell flat on the ground while walking through the city. I had no warning. I was wearing shoes with a platform and I just didn't lift my foot high enough over a raised brick. Have you ever had times when you wanted to fall through the floor and be swallowed whole? It was one of those times. It was so embarrassing. Everyone saw, and I wanted to disappear. I wasn't being careless. It's just that my brain didn't notice what was happening until it was too late, until I was on my face.

Swimming was always dangerous for me. I didn't know which way was up when I went under water. My brain couldn't figure out where the ground or the surface was. Mum would say, "Put your feet down." I would stretch my legs and think I was pushing off the bottom, but I'd still be lying horizontally under the water, madly thrusting my legs in the direction I thought was 'down', looking up at Mum and wondering why I couldn't stand up. As a little kid,

I had to be within arm's reach of an adult at all times. Once, my sister didn't believe Mum when she said I couldn't manage on my own. She told Mum I would be fine, that Mum was just being a 'helicopter parent'. After just half an hour, she came back shaken and said, "You were right. She's got no idea. She's not safe." It was quite humiliating to think that my nephew was a year younger than me and yet he could somehow manage to put his feet down and stand up.

One time in a group swimming class, another kid knocked me off the step, and I started to panic. I didn't know where the edge was or which way was up. The teacher had to lunge across the pool to grab me. After that, it was clear that small group classes just didn't work for me. I needed private lessons with one-on-one attention to keep me safe, and I needed people who understood that my body just didn't give me the same feedback that other kids got.

Crossing roads is terrifying even now. I struggle locating which direction sound is coming from, so I can't always work out where the cars are that I can hear. If there's a slip lane or multiple turning lanes, I can't tell if the road is one way or two ways. Even when I look, I don't always understand what I'm seeing. It feels like guessing and can be dangerous. Carparks are worse. The sounds bounce everywhere. There's engine noise, music, echoing voices, and revving cars, all at once. The hardest part is that I can't tell which cars are moving. If a car has its lights off, I might think it's parked, even if it's about to reverse.

One time, I was almost hit by an electric car. I didn't see or hear it coming. There were no sounds to warn me. I forgot to look. It was another thing to remember when going across the road. My body was busy making sure I didn't fall or trip or bump into anyone or anything. I crossed the road, forgot to look and suddenly there was a loud brake screech. I looked over and the driver saw me just in time. I had come pretty close to dying again. Now I'm extra cautious, but even being cautious doesn't always keep me safe if I can't interpret the sights and sounds around me.

These things don't just make me nervous—they affect my confidence. My independence is really important to me as I get older. I feel anxious in busy places because I don't trust my senses. I don't always know how to stay safe. I have to learn every route, every layout, and every environment by heart. If something changes, I get confused all over again.

Loud environments are very difficult. If there are bright lights, loud sounds, people moving, strong smells, and lots of noise, I can feel completely overwhelmed. It's like all my senses are screaming at me, and I can't filter any of them out. That's when I need to escape. I might run to the toilet, shut myself in a quiet room, or walk away just to get some space. It's not me being dramatic. It's me protecting my nervous system from completely shutting down.

Getting my braces was also a struggle. I already have nerve pain (nociplastic pain) and it means my body can be extra sensitive to touch. When one of the dental assistants started pulling and scraping and really yanking the metal in my mouth, it felt like I was being treated like a medical school mannequin. When you have Sensory Processing Disorder, being rough doesn't just hurt a little—it hurts a lot. After she made me bleed, she had the audacity to blame me and say I wasn't cleaning my teeth properly. Maybe part of the bleeding was from that, but it was also because she was way too rough. That kind of experience doesn't just hurt physically—it makes you feel invisible. You feel like you're not even a person, just a mouth to fix and send away.

I've also noticed that I startle really easily. If someone comes up behind me or talks loudly, I jump. My body reacts before I can even think. And once I'm startled, it takes a long time for me to calm back down. It's not always visible to other people. They don't see the way my heart races or how tense my muscles get. They don't know how long it takes me to recover. But it's real. It affects how I move, how I learn, and how I interact with the world.

I'm learning how to manage my sensory processing struggles more. I use tools like fidgets and sensory toys. I wear soft clothing and avoid tags that itch. I listen to music through one earbud so I can block out some noise without feeling cut off from the world. I use routines to help prepare for what's coming, and I let Mum know when I've had enough and need a break.

What helps most is when people believe me. When they don't tell me I'm overreacting. When they let me step out for a while without making it a big deal. When they understand that I'm not being difficult, that I'm just trying to cope.

Key Takeaways:

Sensory overload is real. It might look like a behaviour problem, but it's actually a physical and emotional reaction to too much input of noise, light, movement, touch or even smell. It's not a choice, and it's not us trying to be difficult. Some kids melt down. Others withdraw and cling to a safe person.

Give children a safe space to retreat when things get too loud, bright, busy, or overwhelming. This might be a quiet corner, a tent, a calming room, or even just a spot where they know it's okay to be alone for a little while. Knowing there's a safe place to go can make a big difference. Being in nature helps me. I love going to the forest area at our local park and just sitting peacefully among the trees or sitting up in the trees. (That's why I created King Jedrik in Sprizzletania. He loves lying in the Fairy Floss Forest.)

Provide calming sensory tools like fidgets, soft textures, headphones, or weighted items to help regulate the nervous system. Let us choose what works best for us. Sometimes our fingers need a certain texture, or our body needs a certain pressure to help us feel okay again.

Use simple, calm voices and give only one instruction at a time. Too much talking or too many directions can make our brains shut down. We might stop responding, not because we're ignoring you, but because we can't process everything at once. If we need to collect a list of items, we cannot remember them all. Just give us one or two at a time or a written list.

Be aware that proprioception issues might cause clumsiness, bumping, or trouble with physical coordination. Please be patient, not critical. We might not even realise we've bumped into someone or dropped something that we thought was put down safely. We're not being careless on purpose. We feel bad when we break things so be gentle with us. I spilt countless drinks thinking I had put them away from the edge of the table or I banged them with my elbow.

Help us learn through repetition, modelling, and kind reminders. Don't assume we'll "just know." Sometimes we need to be shown things again and again in order to feel confident doing them. That's not because we're lazy or defiant. It's just how our brain works. Providing sensory stimuli in controlled environments can help us. Listening to quiet music and sounds in nature, feeling different textures on our bodies and hands, moving our bodies in different ways all helps.

Occupational Therapy can really help. Occupational Therapists are trained to help with sensory issues. They have wonderful activities and can help us develop according to the senses we need. For example, smell wasn't as hard for me as movement. At OT, we would roll, spin, crawl through material tunnels, slide, balance, crash into beanbags... It was great fun while it was helping me develop. I had OT for 10 years, so don't expect a 'quick fix'.

Avoid crowded, noisy places if they are stressful or plan ahead with strategies for breaks, quiet spots, or exits. If we can't avoid them, help us make a plan so we don't become overwhelmed. Prepare us for what to expect where we are going. Knowing there's a way out or a place of safety can reduce a lot of anxiety. Keeping us close to you, holding our hand, putting an arm around our shoulders, giving us noise-cancelling headphones or cuddly sensory fidgets can help. Sometimes we just need to leave and that's okay.

Believe us when we say something is too much. Don't minimise our discomfort. Just because you think it's fine doesn't mean it feels okay to us. Trust us to know our limits. Mum once took me to a Christmas parade. It was supposed to be fun, but the crowds were pressing in on me all around and the noise from the rides and stalls was terrible. People were breathing on me and pushing on me as we wound our way through the crowd. It was overwhelming. I was so scared. I was afraid I would get lost. I was so terrified, I kept tripping on the uneven ground. I started screaming at Mum to wait for me even though she was right there holding my hand as I clung to her shirt. She took me home and sat cuddling me for about half an hour. It was one of those deep pressure, squeezy hugs, still and silent, until I felt safe again.

Let us tell you when we need a break, and don't make us feel bad for needing one. If we ask to step away or take a breather, that's a sign of self-awareness, not misbehaviour. Please support that choice. In class, have a card we can show or a secret sign we can give you if we need to leave.

Support our strengths and help us feel safe, seen, and respected. We're not just a collection of challenges. We have talents, ideas, and potential—and we do best when we feel safe and calm.

20

Literal Interpretation: What Did You Mean?

Being neurodivergent means my brain works a little differently. One of the ways it works differently is that I often take things literally. People say that sometimes, "Oh, you're so literal" However, I don't think most people really understand just how much that affects my everyday life. It's not just about silly misunderstandings or laughing at jokes I don't get. It can cause confusion, frustration, anxiety, and even make me feel like I'm always doing the wrong thing, even when I think I'm doing exactly what was asked.

When a teacher told the whole class to stop talking while we were lining up, I didn't talk. I was completely silent, but I made a little gesture to my friend. I didn't say a word, but the teacher scolded me. I was confused and upset. I followed the rule exactly. It made me scared of getting into trouble because I realised that even when I thought I was doing the right thing, it could still be wrong somehow. Other kids seemed to just *know* what the teacher meant, even when the words weren't exact. I didn't. I needed things to be said very clearly, without assumptions.

When Mum started teaching me at home, she created a research activity she thought would be really fun. She had made a worksheet with questions and had four websites open in different tabs. She explained that one website had information about the government, another had information about the constitution, and so on. She helped me answer the first question using the first website, then said, "Now, finish the worksheet using the four websites to find the information."

It sounded simple enough … to her. When she came back after doing the washing, I hadn't done anything else. I was so angry and frustrated. I was in full meltdown mode. Mum was confused and a bit annoyed. She asked what was wrong, and I shouted, "I can't find it on all four websites!" I thought I had to find the answer to *every single question* on *all four websites*. Not just one. Not pick one. All four. It made perfect sense to my brain the way she said it, but it wasn't what she meant.

There was another time in maths when I was given a question about bus timetables. I had spent a lot of time learning how to interpret visual timetables with Mum's help. It was really hard at first but I finally understood them. The question in the book asked what time I would need to catch the bus to arrive at a place by a certain time. I answered the question by thinking about what I would need to do in real life. I had to allow enough time to get off the bus, find the place, go to the bathroom, locate the room I needed to be in and have time to feel calm, but that wasn't what the question was asking. It wanted the *latest possible time* the bus could get me there, not the real, practical answer I would need. I didn't realise I was doing it "wrong" until my answer was marked incorrect. It made me feel like I just didn't get it. Luckily I was at home and Mum could explain what the writer of the task actually meant. At school, I would have just been marked incorrect and the teachers would assume I couldn't understand the timetable. There would have been no chance to explain my reasoning.

That happens a lot in my life. Literal interpretations can affect so many things: questions on worksheets; things people say; signs on the street. One day we were driving and stopped at a red light. I saw a sign that said "No Standing." I was puzzled and asked Mum, "Why can't you stand on the footpath there?" She laughed and explained it wasn't for pedestrians. It meant cars couldn't park there. So of course, I asked, "Why don't they just say *No Parking* then?" It would make so much more sense.

Literal thinking isn't just a personality quirk. It changes how we see the world. It changes how we understand instructions, rules, jokes, questions, signs—everything. When the world isn't clear, it can make us feel anxious, lost, or even ashamed, but when people take the time to listen to our interpretation, explain things clearly and check we've understood, it makes a huge difference. It helps us feel safer, calmer, and more confident.

Key Takeaways:

Use clear, specific language when giving instructions or asking questions. Vague directions like "no talking" when you really mean no gesturing, mouthing words, touching your friends ... can be confusing. Say exactly what you mean, so we don't get into trouble when we misinterpret your meaning.

Don't assume kids understand what you mean. Check by asking them to explain it in their own words. This makes sure everyone has the same interpretation. Sometimes we nod even when we are confused because we don't want to seem silly. Create an atmosphere where it is okay, even encouraged, to ask questions when we are uncertain.

Be kind and patient if a child misinterprets something. It's not defiance or being 'smart' (and by that I mean a 'smart-alec', not intelligent). It's just how our brain processes information. A misunderstanding doesn't mean we weren't listening. Kindly repeat the instruction and ask us to repeat it. If we still can't understand, maybe try wording it a different way or using a different example, or try using a concrete example we can see.

Avoid idioms or confusing phrases like 'hold your horses' or 'no talking' unless you explain what they mean. Literal thinkers can take things word for word, and phrases like that can cause confusion or even fear. If others laugh at us, or we get into trouble, we lose self-esteem and self-confidence and can either feel angry or withdraw.

Give examples of what you mean when asking a question, especially in tasks or worksheets. A clear example can take away the guesswork and help us understand exactly what you want us to do. Check in to make sure we are on the right track.

If a child seems frustrated or "stuck," try asking what they think the instructions mean. You might find out that we misunderstood something completely. Fixing that misunderstanding can change everything and you might find we actually do understand the concepts, we just became confused when we interpreted the task literally.

Don't punish children for "doing the wrong thing" if they were following what was said, not what was meant. Sometimes we do exactly what we hear, even if it wasn't what the adult intended. That's not defiance—it's literal thinking.

Recognise that literal thinking can lead to anxiety. When we're not sure what something means, it can make us panic or shut down. Please be supportive, not critical.

Praise the effort and problem-solving behind their thinking, even if the answer wasn't quite right. Show us that our thought process matters. It helps build confidence and trust. In the bus timetable problem, Mum was impressed that I had considered allowing time for things like walking to the destination, going to the bathroom and getting a drink when considering which bus I could get to arrive in time. My wrong answer wasn't because I didn't understand the timetable, it was because I was thinking too deeply about the circumstances of the problem.

Help them feel safe to ask questions when something doesn't make sense. If we know we won't be judged for asking, we'll be more likely to speak up instead of silently struggling.

SECTION THREE

Trauma

21

Social and Family Trauma: Where's Home?

Family trauma doesn't always come with bruises. Sometimes it comes with unpredictability, loss and confusion. When I was one year old, my Mum and Dad split up and due to his deception, we lost our house. I didn't know it then, but everything was about to change. For the next nine months, Mum and I were homeless, couch surfing between my sister's place and my Grandparents' house. We were very lucky we had family during this time.

By the time I was two, we were living with my grandparents. My dad wasn't allowed to visit me at home, and I didn't understand why. Why couldn't he live with us? Why couldn't he even come to see me there? Why did Mum always take me to visit him at his motel or a park when he was in Queensland? I had no idea of the pain he had caused my family. Mum didn't want to say anything negative about my Dad to me, but I couldn't let go of the obsession about missing him. I just couldn't understand why my loving, caring family was so against him. It didn't make any sense to me.

Mum was advised by my psychiatrist to simply tell me that Daddy had hurt her so I could move on, but it backfired. In my mind, being hurt meant being hurt physically. Then she had to explain that no, he hadn't hit her or kicked her; he had told lies that hurt our whole family. I still couldn't understand. How could lies hurt someone? I didn't realise how serious it was. I didn't know that his deception, control and financial abuse of Mum had caused us to lose our home. He was the reason we were homeless.

My uncle was another complicated part of my family story. He was an alcoholic, and he was unpredictable. Some days, he was kind and friendly and we would go and visit him. I got to stay over at his house once, and I loved being in the country and playing with the chickens. It felt like a normal, happy time. However, other times, he was completely different. I didn't understand why I could see him one week, but not the next.

One time, he turned up at Grandma's house on his motorbike, dressed all in black. He was immediately abusive to both Grandma and Grandpa so Mum put me straight in the car, and we left. I kept insisting that I wanted to say 'hello' to him. I couldn't understand why I couldn't even see him. Mum just got me to the car. She had to protect me. We spent the next couple of hours sitting in the car at the local shops doing a puzzle book that Mum had just bought me until Grandma rang and told her he had gone and it was safe to go home again.

When I was six, my Grandpa died. He had been like a dad to me. He was my calm, fun person, my safe protector. After he died, everything felt different. There was no buffer any more. My uncle became worse. He started ringing up at all hours of the night, yelling at Mum and Grandma. I didn't understand just how bad the abuse was, so when they hung up on him, I would get really upset ... at them. I thought they were being mean. I'd get mad and yell at them. I didn't understand they were trying to protect me.

I was so afraid of my uncle that I became stressed if I saw men on motorbikes wearing black. One day, I went to the park with Mum, my sister and my nephews. I was riding my bike back, a bit ahead of Mum. I was confident and happy. I could go ahead of Mum because I knew the way ... for once! It was a great day. Suddenly, I was gripped with fear. Coming down the road towards us was a man on a motorbike. He was all in black and his visor was dark as well. He had a balaclava on and I panicked. I froze and stared. I couldn't move at all. The man started slowing as he came nearer. Slower and slower. Suddenly, he was close, right near me, so I dropped my bike, right across a driveway and bolted back to Mum, clinging onto her. My nephews were laughing but I didn't care. I raced to my safe person. It ended up being quite a funny story. The man parked his bike and said, "I'm really sorry. I was just trying to get into my driveway. I didn't mean to scare her." That's how trauma works. One little thing can trigger a fight, flight or freeze response, even though there is actually nothing to be afraid of at that time.

As time went on, things kept getting worse with my uncle. One day, he showed up at our house without warning. Mum acted quickly. She locked me in the back room and told me, "No matter what you hear, you must not come out until I come and get you and tell you it's safe." That was terrifying. I didn't know what was going on. I could hear him yelling, and I wanted to protect Mum and Grandma, but I had to stay hidden. After that, Mum had to go to the doctor and the physiotherapist for a few weeks. I didn't make the connection. I didn't realise he had hurt her while she was trying to protect my Grandma.

Later, when we were moving house, he came to collect his things from the shed. Mum knew it wasn't safe for us to be around him. She took Grandma and me out for the day. We couldn't go home until he had left. Late in the afternoon, we drove past our house but he was still there, so Mum dropped us at my sister's house and kept driving past our place every hour or so, checking over and over again, until she was sure he was gone. We didn't get to go home until it was completely safe, and by then, it was already late.

After we moved, he found where we were. I was petrified. I used to have nightmares about him coming to shoot us. Mum tried to help me by saying that was unlikely but that really didn't help. My fear just kept increasing. The psychiatrist helped instead. She didn't brush my fears aside. She understood. She helped me make a plan just in case something did happen. We planned that if he came, I would go across the road under the guise of having to get something from the lady across the road. I would go over there so I would be safe, and they could ring the police. I appreciated that the psychiatrist understood my need to be prepared. Instead of fearing everything and stressing about the unknown, I had a strategy I could play in my head to be ready. I had a new social script.

Now, sadly, my uncle has alcohol dementia. In some ways, it was the worst thing that could have happened to him, but in other ways, it was also the best. He now lives in a house where he has full-time one-on-one carers around the clock, looking after him. Sometimes I go to visit him, or we invite him to visit us. It's very different now. He doesn't remember us, but he's much safer to be around. When he visits, there's always a carer with him.

I appreciate how lucky I am that I wasn't hurt by anyone physically, but emotional scars are hard to heal. It's hard to trust people.

Key Takeaways:

Children don't always understand the reasons behind family separation or violence. Be clear but age-appropriate when explaining what's happening. Avoid explanations that make things more confusing or scary. We need honesty, but in a way that doesn't overwhelm us.

Try not to criticise the other parent as much as possible. Even if they've caused harm, we might still love them. Hearing bad things about them can be really hard and confusing, especially when we're already trying to make sense of a painful situation.

Predictability helps children feel safe. When people around us are unpredictable, having routines, calm voices, and responses from trusted adults helps us feel less anxious and more secure.

Don't underestimate how children internalise trauma. Sometimes we get upset with the wrong people because we don't yet understand the whole story. Our feelings might come out in different ways, as anger, inappropriate behaviours or withdrawal. Try to recognise our cues and help us deal with our big emotions.

Protective actions like removing a child from a dangerous situation are essential. After the crisis, please explain what happened in a way we can understand. Stick figure drawings or simple stories can help us make sense of it all and begin to feel safe again.

One safe adult can change everything. Even when the rest of the family doesn't feel safe, having just one person who keeps showing up, listens, and cares can be life-changing.

Be patient when children have loyalty conflicts. We might still defend or protect people who have hurt us, not because we're okay with the harm, but because we don't understand it fully. Kind conversations and gentle guidance are important.

Create opportunities for children to talk about their fears. Sometimes talking feels too hard, but drawing, writing, or just having someone listen without judgement can help us process things we don't have words for yet. Movement, play, music and art therapy can be great as we have an outlet for our creativity while we process difficult conversations.

Support visits only when safety is ensured. If a relative seems safer now because of health issues or care changes, we still need protective planning in place. Our emotional safety matters just as much as physical safety.

22

Medical Trauma: The Sharp Sting

Medical trauma has been part of my life for as long as I can remember. Actually, even longer than that—before I could even talk, I was already having things done to my body. For me, hospitals weren't a place I visited once in a while. They were part of my life. Doctors, tests, medications, and fear became normal. But medical trauma isn't just about the actual procedures. It's about how they're done. It's about how it feels to be a child lying on a bed, not knowing what's coming next, and not having the words or the power to say 'no'.

I had open heart surgery at six weeks old and a hernia operation at six months. I had 15 chest infections in one year. I've had six episodes of anaphylaxis—serious, life-threatening allergic reactions. Each one has added another layer to the fear. With every reaction, I've had to race to emergency, get adrenaline, and feel like I'm fighting for my life. The last one was the worst. It required the equivalent of 12 EpiPens before I could breathe properly again. It wasn't just scary. It was terrifying. I didn't know if I was going to survive. It left a mark on me that still hasn't faded.

Then there were all the other things—blood tests, scans, hospital stays, and emergency trips. One of the worst parts wasn't the medical conditions or even the pain. It was being a 'good girl'. I stayed still, even when something hurt. I didn't complain. I didn't scream. I didn't say 'no'. I thought that's what I had to do. I didn't want to be trouble. Inside, I was terrified. I was scared and confused, and I didn't always understand what was happening to me.

When I was very young, about two years old, I was having problems swallowing, so I needed to have a special scan of my throat and stomach. I wasn't prepared for what was to happen. I thought it was going to be the same as the last test I had when I sat in a car seat and they x-rayed me from the side while I ate this horrible contrast. Mum thought it was the same too. How wrong we were!

This was a whole new level of scary. I was expected to lie on a cold, hard, metal table under a very scary black box that looked bigger than me. If that wasn't scary enough, the nurse was shovelling the contrast food into my mouth while I was choking, gagging and crying. She didn't even give me time to try to swallow one bit before she shoved more in. I couldn't keep up with it. I was there because I had swallowing difficulties. Mum tried to get her to stop for a minute so she could give me a quick, reassuring cuddle and give me time to try to swallow a bit sitting up rather than lying flat on my back, but the nurse wouldn't stop. She was very angry, saying she didn't have time for any nonsense as they were already running late. She just kept shoving the contrast into my mouth as I was choking. I was terrified. I was choking and screaming, trying to grab Mum. Mum asked her again to just wait a minute while she calmed me down because I had trouble swallowing and I was choking, but she would not listen. Then the nurse called in reinforcements. She chased Mum out of the way and had about 5 people hold me down, one on each limb as this huge scary box came right down on top of me. I thought it was going to crush me, and all the time, I was coughing and gagging and crying, while the nurse was rousing at me to keep still. Is it any wonder I developed a phobia of medical personnel and medical tests? After that, I learnt to 'keep still' and 'be a good girl' even though what they were doing was hurting me.

When I was six, I detipped my finger and it was terrifying. I slammed the door, and the top of my index finger stayed there while I walked away. Blood was everywhere. Mum yelled out to Grandma to call an ambulance. She had no idea what was happening, but she ran to get the phone while Mum ran to grab a clean tea towel and me. She scooped me up in her arms and cuddled me close while she pressed the tea towel hard on my finger to stop the bleeding. I was in a bit of a daze. I didn't understand what was happening. I kept asking her if I was going to die, and she kept reassuring me, "No, darlin', you'll be okay." But I didn't feel okay. I was very scared.

Mum managed to stop the bleeding, but when we reached the hospital, they tried to X-ray my finger and banged it on the board. Apparently, the blood started pouring out again. The X-ray guy covered the plate with plastic while Mum tried to avert my eyes away from the blood pooling on the floor. She just kept saying it would be okay. Seven hours later, they still couldn't stop the bleeding, so a nurse was instructed to press really hard right on the tip. It was excruciating. I cried out, begging her to stop. I said, "Please stop. Please. It's hurting." Then I turned to Mum and pleaded, "I said please." I couldn't understand why the nurse wouldn't stop when I had asked so nicely. That night, I had to stay in hospital because the next day, I was to have surgery to reattach the tip. After the surgery, I was sent home at 11pm. Mum couldn't believe they were sending us out at that time of night. We had to ring Grandpa to come and collect us because she had come in the ambulance with me. He drove over an hour to collect us. Thank goodness we have been lucky enough to have such a caring family.

Another traumatic experience was the bladder balloon test. I had to go into hospital for a day procedure. They pushed a catheter into me and started filling the balloon. The staff were lovely. They explained what would happen and told me it would feel uncomfortable as it went in. I was told to be a "good girl" and "keep really still." So I did. I didn't want it to hurt too much, but I knew the drill. It felt just like getting a drip. I trusted that they were doing what had to be done. Then they explained that they were going to fill the balloon with water to see how much my bladder would hold. What they didn't explain to me was that I was supposed to tell them when it hurt. I was supposed to know the difference between the discomfort and the pain of my bladder being too full. I didn't know what I was supposed to do—except "keep still and be a good girl." That idea was reinforced when the doctor told me I was doing a great job. So I just lay there. It got more and more painful, but I was "doing great." I didn't say anything. They kept pumping the water in.

After a while, Mum looked over from where she had to sit away from me. She saw a tear rolling down my cheek and asked if I was okay. I didn't know what to say, so she asked again, "Are you all right, darlin'? What's wrong?" I didn't respond. Then she asked, "Is it hurting?" I just nodded. I didn't want to get into trouble. I didn't want to do the wrong thing. I was trying so hard to be a good girl. I was keeping really still. The doctor apologised and said he didn't mean to hurt me. He thought I would have said to stop. But I couldn't say stop. Every time I'd had a test, a drip or a blood test, I had learnt that doctors hurt you.

Growing up with bowel and bladder dysfunction brought its own kind of trauma. I needed nappies well past the age when most kids didn't and that came with teasing. I was told, "Only babies wear nappies" more times than I could count. It made me feel ashamed. I already felt different, and that just made it worse. Once I was sent for an endoscopy and colonoscopy. Mum told the staff that I had been diagnosed with Generalised Anxiety Disorder and PTSD. I would be very scared if I woke up and she wasn't there. They said they would get her in when they could. Mum explained again that she would need to be there as I woke up or I would freak out, but they didn't listen. They had their procedures and parents were not to be allowed in until the anaesthetic had worn off a bit and I had woken up. What a mistake that was!

When I came out of the anaesthetic and Mum wasn't there, I found myself in a strange place surrounded by unfamiliar, scary doctors and nurses. I started screaming, I was absolutely petrified. Mum heard me from out in the waiting room and explained again that she needed to be there, but she was refused entry. For 40 minutes, she had to listen to me screaming from the waiting room, until finally a nurse came out in desperation and said they couldn't calm me and they needed Mum. Mum was so frustrated. When she finally came in, I clung very tightly to her but even the deep pressure cuddles did nothing to calm me. It was another 40 minutes or more before I had calmed enough to stop crying and have a suck of an ice block. My head was pounding. Because they had taken so long, I didn't even have time to finish the ice block before the nurses made us leave as they were getting ready for the afternoon session of patients. I couldn't walk yet, so Mum had to carry me all the way out to the car park. I was about 8 years old, no lightweight, and the car park was about a 15 minute walk from the ward. Poor Mum! I never wanted to have anaesthetic again.

There were so many appointments, so many professionals: gastroenterologists, urologists, paediatricians, GPs, allergists, dermatologists, endocrinologists, psychiatrists, speech therapists, occupational therapists, and psychologists all trying to figure me out. They didn't always agree. I wasn't listening to their arguments, but at each appointment I heard conflicting information about myself. I didn't know who to believe. I didn't know what was actually 'wrong' with me. I was the one stuck in the middle, trying to stay calm while everything felt messy and confusing around me.

Then came one of the scariest medication moments of my life. I had an adverse reaction to fluoxetine. I was playing happily with Mum on holidays when suddenly, I got the most horrific image in my mind—of my head being ripped off. I stopped in the middle of laughing while Mum was tickling me. I couldn't play anymore. It was terrifying. It completely spoiled my day, and long after that, I kept seeing the image in my mind, over and over. When specialists decide to give medicines, they usually weigh up the risks and benefits based on common side effects. But I often get the rare ones. I've had hallucinations from Singulair, a medication for respiratory patients. I've had suicidal ideations from Keppra, the epilepsy medicine. Horrific images from fluoxetine. Joint pain from Dupixent. Not to mention all the other allergies to medicines that caused rashes, severe stomach upsets, and even splits in my fingertips. The list goes on. Having any new medicine is very scary. I never know how my body will react.

Each medical experience added a new layer to my trauma. It built up over time. One appointment might seem small to someone else, but to me, it was another reminder that my body didn't feel like it was mine. The more I went through, the harder it became. I started becoming more and more anxious around doctors. Then, I had an awesome GP who understood me. He gently tried to overcome my fears. He would tickle me or just listen to my chest and send me home, but he made it a joke, laughing about the cold stethoscope, pretending to put it on himself and shivering before warming it up for me. That really helped me.

As I got older, I began to change. I started speaking up. I began asking questions with Mum's encouragement. I told nurses to check ingredients, especially because of my allergies. I couldn't risk someone getting it wrong. I had to learn to be my own advocate, even as a kid. I learned that staying quiet wasn't always safe. I learned that being a 'good girl' didn't protect me. What helped was speaking up, even if my voice was shaking. What helped was having adults who listened when I finally did speak.

It's still hard. I still struggle with medical trauma. It doesn't just disappear because I'm older now. It's in my body, and my brain remembers everything, even if others have forgotten. Now I understand it better. I don't feel dramatic for being scared. I know it's real. I know it makes sense. I'm not broken—I'm someone who's been through a lot and is still learning how to live with it. Now I can be a voice for those young children who cannot speak up for themselves. I can be their advocate.

Key Takeaways:

Don't assume silence means they're okay. Just because a child is quiet or compliant doesn't mean they aren't scared. Ask questions gently and watch for non-verbal cues.

Be honest about what will happen. Tell the child step by step what you are going to do. If possible, do it to their toy first, read a book about it or let them see a video of the procedure they are going to have that has been specially prepared for children (not the gory ones!).

Make sure the child understands what is expected of them. Don't just tell them what *you're* going to do: tell them what *they* need to do. If they're supposed to say when something hurts, explain that clearly. I once came out of the doctor's surgery and told Mum the doctor really hurt my tummy. She said, "Why didn't you tell him? That's why he was pressing, to see where it hurt." I replied that I thought I had to be a good girl and keep still like when they hurt me putting the drip in my arm.

Use clear language for kids who take things literally. Don't use phrases like "a little sting" or "this won't take long" unless you explain what that really means. What is a 'little' sting? How long will it take? 2 seconds, 5 minutes? Keep it simple and explain why you need to do this and how it will help.

Reassure without minimising. Comfort them with kindness and honesty. Don't say, "It won't hurt," if it will. Say, "I know this will hurt a bit, but Mummy is right here. Would you like to hold her hand?"

Teach and model consent. Let them know they have a right to understand, ask questions, and say if something doesn't feel okay.

Help them feel in control. Little choices like choosing to lie down or sit in the chair, choosing which arm to use for a test, or bringing a comforting toy, can help the child feel some control over their world and their body.

Prepare for medications carefully. If a child has experienced scary side effects before, take time to talk about new medications and watch closely for reactions.

Trust their instincts. If a child says something doesn't feel right, take it seriously, even if the medical staff think it's fine.

Normalise speaking up. Praise bravery not just for staying still, but also for saying, "That hurts," or "I need a break."

Support their emotional recovery after procedures. Let them talk, cry, draw, or play it out. Trauma can linger, even if the physical pain stops.

Allow sufficient time for appointments so kids don't feel pressured to keep your schedule. Allowing time for a child to calm down can be more time efficient in the long run instead of trying to do a test on a screaming, petrified child.

Be their advocate. Step in when they can't. If they're frozen or unsure, be the one who helps their needs be met and their voice be heard.

Be patient and compassionate. Understand what it must be like for the scared child who has no experience with what you do every day. A little kindness goes a long way.

Use humour to lessen the stress. Playing with the cold stethoscope, making hand puppets with the medical gloves ... all these little things make a difference to a frightened child.

23

Owning My Body: Power Imbalance

Body autonomy is often talked about when it comes to sex education or reproductive rights, which is important, but for me (and for so many others who've shared their stories with me) it's something that was stripped away over and over again during my medical journey. Most of the time, the medical or mental health professionals didn't even realise they were crossing a line because they were doing the same things every day.

Every test is different and no one prepares you for what's going to happen. You just get told what to do and where to lie, or worse, you're not told anything at all. In any other situation, the things that happen in hospitals would be seen as assault. If someone gassed you on the street without telling you what was in the mask, if they stuck needles in your body without your 'okay', put balloons or instruments inside your genitals without your consent or watched you undress, people would call the police. However, when it happens in a hospital, it's called "treatment."

It doesn't feel like care. It feels like a hostage/assault situation. Multiple strangers crowd around and hold you down. They are not holding a knife. Instead, they have a sharp needle with unknown substances inside. Medical teams say they are going to do something, and you feel compelled to say 'yes' even though the needle is a threat. It becomes a weapon in a place that is supposed to be safe. It is like you're at knife point and no one is explaining anything. Of course we cry. Of course we fight. That's not being difficult. That's fear. That's what happens when our nervous system senses danger. We're not saying 'no' because we are being stubborn or just because we want to be difficult. We are saying 'no' because we are terrified. We are scared of being hurt. What if someone paused for a moment and took the time to calm us down? What if they reassured us that we were safe? I promise you, those appointments would go ten times faster and be a lot less traumatic than holding us down while we kick and scream.

People always say, "There's no excuse for abuse." But what about us? What about when six or seven doctors and nurses are impatient with you, raising their voices at you, holding you down, and putting needles in you? Why isn't that seen as abuse too?

I am not saying that medical tests and procedures aren't important. I completely understand that sometimes they are the only way to save someone's life. But what I am asking is: is it really consent if we don't even know what we're consenting to? Isn't consent when you can make an informed decision? Saying "yes" when you don't understand what's happening isn't true consent. It's something else. It's pressure. It's fear. It's people-pleasing, and a lot of that behaviour comes from trauma and people brushing your consent aside.

A lot of the time, I felt like I had to say "yes" because it's the doctor or because Mum told me I could trust doctors or I didn't want to get into trouble. Now I realise that those "yeses" and timid "okays" weren't always real. They were survival. They were trauma responses. They were part of a much bigger issue that needs to be talked about more: body autonomy in the medical world. Where can we all do better? How can we limit trauma responses?

There was one time, when I had full-body eczema, and the hospital needed to take progress photos during a three-day intensive treatment that a male medical photographer had to take pictures of me stripped from head to toe. I have had to do this before in front of many doctors, nurses and students which was uncomfortable, but this time, I had to have photos taken of my skin from head to toe to monitor my progress. Mum had to have a long, in-depth conversation with me afterwards about how *no person should ever take photos of me like that*—except in this one very specific, medical situation. In any other situation, it would have been a terrible, unsafe thing, but because it happened in a hospital, it was "normal." That was really hard for me to understand when I was younger. How can something be wrong everywhere else but somehow okay just because it's behind hospital walls?

Even the words professionals use can make a big difference. Don't just say, "Can you pull your pants down?" That makes me freeze. That makes my brain go, "Wait—why? What are you going to do to me?" Instead, say something like: "Can you pull your pants down for me? I'd like to check how your [body part] is looking, so I can adjust your treatment if we need to. **I'll let you know before I do anything else.** Right now, I just want to take a look." That would get a much more confident "Okay." Not the hesitant

"...okay..." with a pause. Those hesitant "okays" with silence and confusion? They are not consent. They are a silent plea for more information. Ensure you only do what you say you are going to do. If you say you are just going to take a look, only take a look that time. Do not continue and start treatment after just saying you are going to take a look because you will break our trust immediately. Before you do anything, make sure we know we can stop you at any time, that we can ask questions. And please mean it. Be genuine. Use a gentle tone to show us you care, because if you don't, we remember, not just in our brains, but in our bodies. It takes years to heal from that.

With my psychologist, I had a moment where I realised something important: my body autonomy was ignored when I was younger. Even though I understand that in emergencies, consent might look different, it still feels wrong. It feels like something precious was taken. I'm starting to explore what true consent really means. People say you can set your boundaries, but if I don't even know what's going to happen, or what is expected of me, how can I know what my boundaries are? How can I know if what you're doing is okay? Being neurodivergent doesn't help either since I have difficulty interpreting people's cues.

To heal from some of those scary experiences, I've had to move my body and reconnect with it. I've had to show myself that *I* am in control now. *I* own my body. My body is mine. But sometimes, it still feels like part of me was taken away. Those medical professionals took something—my choice, my power—and I didn't even realise it at the time. It made me feel like a victim. Like my body didn't belong to me any more.

Key Takeaways:

Explain everything before it happens. Don't assume the child knows what to expect. Use simple, clear words. Tell them exactly what will happen, in what order, and **why**.

Don't just ask for a yes—make sure it's a real yes. A quiet, mousy or confused "... okay ..." isn't consent. If the child looks unsure, stop and check in. Ask, "Do you want me to tell you more about what I'm going to do?"

Let them know they can say "no" or stop things. Make it clear that they have the power to pause or say "no" at any point and mean it. If they say "stop," actually stop. Make sure there is sufficient appointment time to enable patience and calm. Sometimes a child just needs a little reset before continuing. A little cuddle, a quick drink can make all the difference. Rushed, stressed children will 'fight' more (that fight or flight mode), and that will take so much longer.

Use gentle, respectful language. Don't just say "pull your pants down." Instead, explain why and what you'll do. Say something like, "I need to check your skin to help with your treatment. Is it okay if I have a look now?"

Always get permission first, even in small things. Ask before touching, taking photos, or starting a procedure, even if you think it's minor. It shows respect and gives the child a sense of control and body autonomy.

Check your tone. A calm, kind, genuine voice helps the child feel safe. Rushing or sounding impatient makes it feel like danger, not care. We feel unseen and unheard.

Respect the child's boundaries, even if they can't say them. If a child is frozen, crying, or backing away, something doesn't feel right to them. Slow down. Reassure them. Don't push ahead because you are strapped for time.

Never confuse compliance with consent. Just because a child says "yes", stays quiet, or follows instructions doesn't mean they feel okay about what you are about to do. Sometimes they are responding out of fear or are people-pleasing.

Sometimes there are emergencies, tests or procedures you need to do that a child doesn't want. When that happens, take the time to explain what you are doing and why as you do it. Use a calm tone and reassure them as you proceed. Apologise and explain that you understand the child doesn't want this, but it really is important for whatever reason. Do the procedure and prep slowly if possible and always speak calmly instead of being angry and impatient.

Support children after uncomfortable situations. Talk about what happened. Let them ask questions. Let them know it's okay to feel upset, scared, or confused. Help them process it.

Remind them their body belongs to them. Say it out loud: "You're the boss of your body. You can tell us what to do. What would you like to happen?" "You get to say what happens to it." Even in medical care, kids need to hear that message.

Be careful with mixed messages. Be careful with terms like "Be a good girl." If something is okay in hospital but not okay anywhere else (like being undressed in front of adults), talk through it. Explain the difference clearly so the child isn't left confused or unsafe in other situations. This is especially important for neurodivergent children who have difficulty knowing what to do in different social situations.

Be trauma-informed, not forceful. Holding a child down isn't just distressing: it can feel like assault. Avoid it unless it's a genuine emergency and always explain what's happening and why if restraint is absolutely necessary.

Remember medical trauma is real. Just because it's a hospital doesn't mean it's not scary. The child's brain and body respond to fear the same way, whether it's a stranger on the street or a nurse with a needle.

Validate the child's emotions. Say things like, "I know this is scary," or "You're allowed to feel scared." Don't brush off their fear. Help them feel seen and heard.

Give them control wherever you can. Let them choose which arm for the blood test, whether they sit or lie down, or who is in the room. Small choices can make a big difference.

Model consent in every interaction. Even if the child is nonverbal or very young, always ask, always explain, always include them in the process.

Understand that one negative experience can cause lasting trauma. Try to make every interaction as gentle as possible. You don't know everything the child in front of you has gone through.

Understand that healing takes time. Your respectful, informed approach now might be the first step in helping that child feel safe again and know that their consent is valid.

24

Lack of Awareness In Our Community

Sometimes, the hardest part of trauma isn't the trauma itself. It's the way people react to it. The way they talk about it, or ignore it. The way they dismiss it, minimise it, or judge it. It's the way people act like they know what trauma is when they've never really lived it. Or worse, when they act like someone else's trauma doesn't count. I've seen it happen, not just to me, but to the kids I meet.

I remember this one day so clearly. I was talking with a little girl I worked with. We weren't even having a deep conversation. We were just chatting and sharing stories about Our Pixie Friends and how the characters helped her feel less alone when an older lady came up to us. The little girl, being brave and open, said, "I've had trauma," because we were already talking about it. She wasn't trying to get attention. She was just being real. She was being vulnerable. She was showing courage.

And then the lady said something that made my stomach drop.

She looked the girl straight in the eyes and said, "What would you know about trauma?"

She didn't even hesitate. There was no kindness, no compassion, just judgement. She had no idea what that little girl had been through. She wasn't aware that her dad had taken his own life. That little girl lived through so much pain, so much confusion. She has complex PTSD, even if she doesn't fully understand what that means yet. And here was someone making her feel like she didn't have a right to her story. Like her trauma wasn't real enough. Like she wasn't allowed to speak.

That moment stuck with me. It's one of those moments you don't forget, because it showed me just how powerful people's attitudes can be: how they can either lift someone up or crush them completely. And that's why I needed to write this chapter. Trauma isn't always visible. You can't always tell by looking at someone what they've been through. Just because someone is smiling or functioning doesn't mean they aren't carrying a heavy load.

There is this culture now, especially online, where people make jokes about trauma. Memes and comments like "I'm so traumatised" are thrown around about anything and everything. And yeah, I get it. Sometimes people use humour to cope. I've done it too. But there's a big difference between laughing at something you've been through to survive it, and using the word "trauma" so casually that it loses its meaning. I've seen jokes about having allergies and anaphylaxis. I'm sure if those people had a family member who had experienced anaphylaxis, they wouldn't be so quick to make fun of those who live with that fear every day. For people with real trauma—the kind that affects you every single day—it's not funny. It's not a joke. It's real. It's raw. It's painful. And it deserves to be respected.

I've learned there's a difference between being *anxiety-aware* and *trauma-aware*. Being anxiety-aware means you know about anxiety. You know what it looks like. You might recognise it in yourself or in others. Being trauma-aware is deeper. It means you understand that certain things, sometimes seemingly small things, can be massive triggers for someone with trauma. Things like a smell, a sound, a person, a place or even a colour. A motorbike backfiring, loud footsteps, people drinking alcohol are all things that can trigger fearful responses depending on people's traumatic experiences. The way someone looks at you, the tone in their voice, a smelly hospital corridor. It doesn't always make sense to anyone else, but it doesn't have to.

Trauma lives in the body. It hides in the nervous system. So even when you're technically safe, you don't *feel* safe. And when someone brushes that off, when they say you're just being dramatic or too sensitive, it cuts deeply. It makes you question yourself. It makes you feel like maybe it's *you* who's the problem.

I've been there. I've had people say, "You're too young to know what trauma is." I've had people roll their eyes when I've told them I have PTSD. I've had people dismiss my story because I'm still here, I'm still breathing and because I'm still smiling. But here's the truth. You can smile and still be hurting inside. You can laugh and still feel like the world is crumbling. You can survive the worst things imaginable and still look like you are coping. You can appear "fine" on the outside.

I want to ask you something. I want to ask you to do one thing today. Just one thing to help someone feel safe. Not just feel physically safe, but feel *emotionally safe, psychologically safe.* Maybe that means not hugging someone. Maybe it means giving them space. Maybe it means listening without interrupting. Maybe it means asking, "What do you need right now?" instead of assuming you know. Maybe it means not making jokes about trauma just because it's trendy. Maybe it means saying, "I do believe you," even when you don't fully understand. Maybe it's as simple as saying, "I see you. I hear you. I'm not going anywhere. I'm here for you."

Creating safety doesn't have to be big. Sometimes the smallest gestures make the biggest difference, because when someone feels safe, they can start to heal, even just a little. And sometimes, that little bit of healing is enough to help them keep going.

Key Takeaways:

Believe their story, even if it surprises you. Never question a child's experience just because they are young. If they open up about trauma, listen with respect, not doubt.

Don't judge what you can't see. Trauma isn't always visible. Kids can laugh, smile, and still be in pain. Just because they're functioning doesn't mean they are fine.

Avoid minimising language. Phrases like "It's not that bad," "You're too sensitive," or "You'll get over it" are harmful. Instead, say things like, "That sounds really hard," or "I'm here if you need to talk."

Be careful with the word "trauma." Avoid casual jokes or memes about trauma in front of children with real traumatic histories. It can feel dismissive or invalidating.

Respect their triggers. Don't argue with a child about what "should" or "shouldn't" be upsetting. Triggers can seem small to others but are very real to the person experiencing them. Seeing a man wearing black and riding a motorbike was enough to trigger my freeze response.

Don't force physical touch. Ask for permission before hugging or touching. For some kids, physical contact can feel unsafe or triggering, depending on their experiences.

Let them set the pace. Allow the child to share when they are ready. Don't push for details or expect them to explain everything.

Ask, don't assume. Instead of deciding what support the child needs, ask them. "Would you like to talk?" "Do you want some quiet time?" or "How can I help you right now?" Giving them some control can go a long way towards healing.

Create psychological safety. This means making kids feel like they're seen, heard, and supported. Say things like "You're not alone," or "I believe you."

Be trauma-aware, not just anxiety-aware. Learn what trauma really looks like and how it shows up in kids' bodies, behaviours, and emotions so you can respond in a way that helps, not harms.

Let every child know, through your words and actions, that they matter. Their story matters, and they don't have to carry their pain alone.

SECTION FOUR

Strategies For Age Groups

25

Strategies for Ages 0-2

This was the beginning of everything—before I even had words. So much was already happening inside my body and brain. I had traumatic medical procedures, breathing problems, surgery, infections, and early signs of anxiety. The things that helped me most weren't complicated. They were simple, gentle, and full of love.

However, some things didn't help at all. In fact, some things made everything worse for me. Even though I couldn't say it at the time, my body remembered. Now I can look back and tell you what helped and what didn't, based on what my family and I noticed.

Helpful Strategies

These are the things that made a real difference in helping me feel safe, calm, and connected, even though I couldn't explain what I was feeling at the time. They may not work for every child. Every person is different.

Physical comfort and connection

Lots of cuddles and reassurance. I was comforted by physical closeness. It helped regulate my breathing and heart rate. I had lots of cuddles with other safe people too. My grandparents gave me comfort, love, and stability, especially in those early months when life felt overwhelming. Grandpa gave the best back scratches. He applied pressure whereas Mum was too gentle.

Mum took 3 months off work as advised by the psychiatrist. Having her with me every day gave me consistency and security when everything else felt scary and confusing.

Falling asleep in Mum's arms. I often threw up before bed, and then I'd fall asleep being held. That helped me calm down after such stressful evenings.

Being held tightly with pressure. Deep pressure helped my nervous system settle. Even though I didn't have the words for it, it felt safe. Sometimes I needed to be held for up to 40 minutes with no movement—no rocking or swaying—and totally silent. No shushing or singing either. Just stillness. What helped most depended on my mood.

Understanding my needs

Circle of Security. This was a turning point for Mum. It helped her understand that when I needed her close by, that was okay. Mum knew that although other people thought she was being a "helicopter parent," she knew it was what I needed, so she ignored their comments and did what was best for me and my development. (https://www.circleofsecurityinternational.com/pages/what-is-the-circle-of-security)

Hand Model of the Brain. Daniel Siegel's hand model helped Mum understand that my brain wasn't just overreacting—it was doing what it thought it needed to survive. My amygdala was always firing off, sending danger signals, even when things weren't dangerous. This helped Mum realise I couldn't settle or learn or listen until I felt safe again. I needed help calming my brain before anything else could happen. (https://drdansiegel.com/hand-model-of-the-brain/)

Healing time and gentle introduction to the world

When I first came home from the premmie nursery at three months old, I wasn't allowed in public because my immune system wasn't very well developed. It was isolating for Mum, but it helped give me time to heal instead of getting sick again.

Once I was able to start going out, we went to lots of parks and had little adventures in the pram. I loved the fresh air and the movement of the pram. At home, I spent time outside playing on the grass and feeling the breeze and sunshine.

Sensory and movement experiences

I had lots of sensory experiences early on. Feeling different textures, crawling through my little tunnel and tent, touching cool hard tiles and snuggling into soft blankets were all necessary to help my nervous system develop.

By the time I was two, I was being brushed with a therapy brush to help develop and regulate my nervous system. These small but consistent sensory supports really made a difference in how my body processed the world.

I attended occupational therapy from early on in my life. Lots of sensory skills were developed with their help, and I am extremely grateful to them.

Language and connection through play

Even in the NICU, Mum would read and sing to me. It was important to help develop my language skills, even though I was so little.

When we came home, we kept reading every day. We sang, laughed, and played together. These moments weren't just fun: they helped my brain grow and helped me feel connected to family.

Consistency and predictability

Familiar routines at home helped. When the outside world felt chaotic, having predictable routines at home (same cuddles, same bathing and bedtime procedures) helped reduce my stress.

Unhelpful Strategies

Even though people meant well, these things made me more anxious or overwhelmed at this age:

Inconsistency

I had one daycare mum who was lovely, but when I started chanting "Mummy, Mummy" all day long after my dad left and we were homeless, she didn't know what to do. She tried cuddling me. She tried putting me on the mat. She tried ignoring me. She even tried rousing at me. The inconsistency didn't help, because nothing was predictable. I didn't know how she was going to respond, and that made it even harder for me to feel safe.

Not having a stable home was difficult. We were at my sister's house from Monday to Thursday night, then at my grandparents' house from Friday to Sunday night. During the week, I was at the day care lady's house. I didn't know where I was going to be. That lack of stability made it hard to settle and feel secure.

Adults hiding emotions

Mum was hiding how she felt. Even though she thought she was protecting me, I could sense something wasn't right. When adults pretend everything is fine, I get more anxious because their faces don't match their emotions. That may even be part of the reason I have difficulty understanding social cues now. My baby brain was mirroring her brain, but when she was feeling upset or sad, she was putting on a brave face and a smile, which was inconsistent. I learned to trust faces that didn't always match feelings, and that made it confusing later on when reading people's emotions.

Exposure to unpredictable fears

When we were homeless and couch surfing between my sister's place and my grandparents' house, my sister had a crazy, unpredictable, very energetic dog. Because I never knew what it was going to do or when it was going to run over me, I was petrified. I couldn't relax. Being around something unpredictable just kept my nervous system on high alert.

Even at this age, my nervous system was already on high alert. The things that helped most were about safety, connection, predictability, and understanding. I didn't need fancy strategies—I needed people to slow down, stay close, and help me feel safe in my body and in the world.

26

Strategies for Ages 2-5

This was a time when I was learning to do more things but also feeling a greater range of emotions. My anxiety and sensory issues were becoming more obvious, but people didn't always understand what was going on. I didn't have the words to explain it all, so I used behaviours, repetition, or told people my finger hurt when I was feeling overwhelmed.

There were some helpful strategies and some that just didn't work for me at all.

It was important that my whole team worked together. My mum worked closely with my psychiatrist, psychologist, OT, speech therapist, teachers, medical practitioners, and specialists. Everyone respected the important role Mum played in helping me, because they only saw me for an hour at a time but she was with me so much more. They explained things to Mum so she could support me at home and in daily life. It also helped that she was a trained special education teacher. Mum was aware of developmental stages and was aware of things I did that didn't quite seem right. Because of her observations, I was able to get early intervention from speech therapists to help me with swallowing and speaking and occupational therapists that helped me with my sensory needs and fine and gross motor skills.

Helpful Strategies

Visual schedules

My OT made me a visual schedule using Velcro-backed pictures on a board. As we finished each task, we moved the picture to the other side. It helped me know what was happening now, what we would be doing next and when we would be finished. I had input into choosing the tasks which helped me feel I had some choice and control.

We used visual schedules at home too, for morning and evening routines. As I got older, I'd forget to move the pictures, so it only worked when someone helped me step by step.

Social stories and books

Social stories helped me prepare for new situations, like Kindy or the doctor. They were also really useful after something had happened—like going to hospital. We would draw stick figures, cartoon-style, as we told the story together to help me process what I'd just been through.

Reading books about new experiences helped me to prepare for life experiences like birthday parties, moving house and going to the doctor or dentist. We would read and reread about them before and after events. *The Little Book of First Experiences* by Anne Civardi was a great resource.

The Kissing Hand by Audrey Penn was used at Kindy. We painted handprints, laminated them and took them home for our mums to kiss with bright lipstick. We brought them back to Kindy, and when we missed our mums, we could take the handprint from our locker and put it on our cheek. I used mine a lot.

The Invisible String by Patrice Karst helped me feel connected to Mum even when we were apart.

It's Okay to Be Different by Todd Parr helped me feel like being different wasn't wrong: it was just part of who I was. Books like this made me feel seen and accepted.

We read books about emotions and books that reminded me how much Mum loved me, no matter where I was.

We also talked a lot, read books and sang songs about how God and Jesus always love me, no matter what. That helped me feel safe and loved even when everything around me felt confusing.

I also did meditation and relaxation strategies with storybooks and CDs. One was about the Indigo Fairy relaxing into a flower. As the petals closed over the fairy's limbs in the story, Mum would gently place soft coral fleece over that part of my body. It helped me feel safe and calm. This strategy came from my psychiatrist.

My psychologist taught me how to reframe my thoughts using red and green Duplo blocks. She'd place a red block and say, "Oh no, Mummy has left me at Kindy." Then I'd replace it with a green block and say, "But it's okay. She'll be back."

Advance warning for transitions

Mum would say things like, "You've got 5 minutes left to play." I couldn't tell time, but it helped me understand something was about to change which gave me time to prepare.

Safe goodbye rituals and predictable routines

We had a consistent goodbye routine when Mum dropped me off. Doing it the same way each time made it feel more okay. One morning when Mum dropped me at Prep, I started crying and couldn't stop. The Prep aide ran down to the carpark to get Mum. When she came back, I told her she had forgotten to give me a kiss. She reminded me she had, but I cried, "It wasn't a squeaky one!" Even the little details were very important to me.

I felt safer when I knew what was coming next. Having a regular bedtime routine with bath, eczema creams, books, cuddles and bed gave me some of the stability I needed.

Safe, familiar adults

I couldn't cope with relief teachers or unfamiliar people. If my teacher was away, I would be taken to a classroom with a familiar teacher, or the special needs teacher would look after me.

Teachers would always keep me close. If we were doing something new or going anywhere, even just to a different part of the school or another classroom, they would hold my hand or let me sit in their laps.

They used the Circle of Security model. My Kindy teacher was amazing. If I wasn't coping, even at lunchtime or after school care, she would come back to support me, leaving staff meetings or cutting her own lunch short. She genuinely cared.

I stayed in Kindy with her for two years so I didn't have to transition to a different teacher when I repeated. That stability, at home and at Kindy, really helped me flourish.

Repeating Kindy was celebrated at my school. The head of Early Years came around with an official-looking folder and said she was choosing special children to become "Kindy Leaders." I was so excited to be chosen! At the end-of-year Kindy graduation, we got to go on stage and receive a special crown. It made us feel really important and valued. The only problem was that I took the role very seriously. By June the next year, my teacher had to have a special meeting with Mum to let me know I didn't have to be a Kindy Leader anymore because I was getting stressed trying to teach the other children how to behave!

I had a safe and gentle GP who helped me build trust by taking things slowly. Sometimes, I would come into the room just to talk and be tickled and then leave without anything happening. On another visit, he used the stethoscope as part of a game, trying it out on my toy first, then listening to my chest and joking about how cold it was before he warmed it up.

The dentist also made me feel safe. She let me come and have a ride in the magic chair and showed me her fairy room. I didn't even have to open my mouth at first. On another visit, I let her count my teeth and then went home.

These little steps helped me build trust with safe people and overcome my fears. They were extremely important, especially because I'd had so many traumatic medical experiences already.

Supported transition into daycare

Before I started daycare, my psychiatrist went to the centre to talk to the staff and explain the trauma I had experienced, which helped them understand what kind of support I would need. To help me transition, Mum and I started by staying for just one hour, with me sitting on her lap the whole time. Over the next few days, I gradually moved a little further away from her, while she stayed within sight, helping in the classroom. Slowly, she began stepping out of the room for short periods, starting with just ten minutes, then longer. By the third week, I was able to stay for the whole day without her. I didn't realise how important that gentle transition was at the time, but I'm so thankful now. It helped me feel safe and secure with new adults because everyone worked together as a team to support me.

Deep pressure play and sensory calming

My OT taught us lots of deep pressure activities. One of my favourites was called *'sausage roll'*. If I was having a meltdown, was very stressed, or upset, Mum would lie me on the bed on top of my soft blanket and wrap me up like a sausage roll as I rolled over and over until I was tightly wound in the blanket. Then she'd playfully pretend to put tomato sauce on me, wiping with deep pressure down my back and legs and "gobble me up."

We also played *'pizza'*. Mum would do different sensory activities for each topping. She would wipe down my body for the sauce, tap all over my back to add ham or pineapple, and press gently down on my back for the cheese. It always ended with "eating" me, "Yum, yum, yum!" The humour always broke the tension, and by the end, I would be laughing instead of having a meltdown.

The healing power of humour and play

Humour was a big part of my healing. Grandpa was always doing funny things like pretending to give me the *Royal Order of the Chilly Tootsy* by putting my foot under the cold tap or dressing me up in his great big fireman pants.

We had lots of tickles and pretend play. One year when I figured out who Santa was, I spent three months role-playing with Mum, practising sitting on Santa's knee and having conversations. We did it over and over—at least a hundred times—and Mum was always patient. She understood that repetition was how I processed events and social interactions.

Movement helped me process

My OT gave me lots of sensory and motor activities. I loved sitting in the sand and searching for hidden toys, balancing on stepping stones while trying to catch a ball, walking along a low beam, and hanging from the big triple-layered hammock. I even learned to sit, lie, and stand on the log swing. The scooter board was a bit scary at first, but I loved crashing into the big beanbags at the end! OT felt like fun and it was helping me develop and regulate at the same time.

My psychiatrist also understood that I needed to move to process big feelings. I would be doing gymnastics while she talked, and Mum thought I was being rude. But the psychiatrist reassured her that I *was* listening. The content was just hard, and moving helped me cope. That was all new for Mum, but it changed the way she supported me.

Allergy awareness and safety

My Kindy was really good at making sure I was safe. They read books to the class about having allergies so everyone could understand. They made new rules like kids having to wash their hands before and after eating, and teachers wiped down the computers and surfaces regularly. When I reacted to the toilet cleaner, the teacher made sure the aide wiped it down again with safe products. That made a big difference and helped me feel cared for.

Facing new experiences with support

Even though I was anxious about new experiences like birthday parties or horse rides, Mum never let me avoid them. Instead, she supported me so I could cope. She would prepare me in advance, role-play what might happen, stay close so I felt secure, and reassure me while I was there. Afterwards, we would retell the event to Grandma and Grandpa, which helped me feel proud and build confidence. Avoiding the experience might have made things worse, but Mum's approach helped me grow.

Outdoor play and motor planning

Mum bought lots of outdoor play equipment for me—ramps, trestles, and climbing frames. She would help me with motor planning to figure out how to use them. I spent many hours learning by rote where to place my hands and feet so I could climb, balance, and move safely. But if Mum moved the equipment, even just rotated it, she would have to start teaching me all over again. The change confused me, and I couldn't transfer the same skills to the new setup unless we practised it step by step again. It took a lot of effort, but it helped me learn to play more easily.

Unhelpful Strategies

Being misunderstood as 'dobbing'

Sometimes I would tell the teacher when another child did something unsafe. I wasn't trying to get them into trouble. I was just really anxious about someone getting hurt or doing something wrong. I needed things to be safe. But people thought I was "dobbing" and didn't understand what was going on for me.

Unsafe allergy environments

One time, I was seated at a table with a child who didn't understand my allergies. They waved peanuts in my face. It was really scary and dangerous. That situation didn't help me feel safe at all.

Not being prepared for new or scary things

No preparation for unfamiliar places or events was stressful. When I was taken somewhere new and no one explained it or prepared me, I panicked. Even smells or sounds I didn't expect could send me into a meltdown.

Surprises felt terrifying – Even good surprises could feel like danger to my nervous system. I didn't like being startled.

I didn't always know how to say what I needed, but my body and behaviour said it for me. Strategies like visual supports, books, deep pressure play, gentle transitions, humour, movement, and having safe people around made a huge difference. When routines changed or people misunderstood me, it made everything harder.

27

Strategies for Ages 5–10

Ages 5 to 10 were harder for me. A lot of big things happened during this time. My Grandpa died when I was six, I had more scary medical procedures, and I was still dealing with lots of different types of anxiety. I was diagnosed with PTSD at 6, and later on, by the time I was 9, depression too.

At school, things got more confusing. I didn't understand my work sometimes, especially in maths and science, and I found it really hard to interpret people's faces and social cues. That made me anxious. I had never struggled with the work before. I didn't realise that my NVLD made comprehending abstract concepts difficult and at school around the ages of 8-9 is the time kids move from the 'learning to read' phase to the 'reading to learn' phase, when inferential comprehension really becomes important. I couldn't interpret people's cues in person, so I certainly couldn't interpret their cues on the page if they were being sarcastic or the literal interpretation didn't make sense. I often felt scared of getting into trouble, even when I wasn't doing anything wrong. It wasn't until I was 9 that I was finally diagnosed with NVLD, and that was hard to accept. I was going to have to live with this for the rest of my life.

People didn't always understand that my reactions came from anxiety or that my NVLD made things harder. There were times when things were overwhelming and I didn't know how to ask for help properly. But there were also some really helpful strategies that made a difference: things that helped me feel safe, calm, and understood. There were also strategies that didn't help at all. Some of them made things worse. I want to share both because everybody is different and what didn't help me, may help someone else.

Helpful Strategies

Daily support and preparation for school

A teacher aide met me every morning to help me settle. She was calm, gentle, and familiar. Starting the day with her helped me regulate my emotions and feel safe. We used a special notebook filled with positive affirmations. Just reading through kind, encouraging words helped me believe I could get through the day.

I had multiple visits with my new teacher at the end of the school year while my familiar, safe teacher was also present. Then, before school started, I would meet with them again. I was shown the new classroom so I could begin to familiarise myself with the new environment before any other kids were there so it was less overwhelming. I could also start to learn new routes such as from the car to the new classroom block. Then from the classroom to the toilets, or the office. These early meetings helped reduce my anxiety about the unknown and made the first day much less scary.

Trusted people and safe places

I had soft toys like Worry Bunny and my Fairy Dream Maker. They weren't just toys. They helped me feel safe, grounded, and comforted during tough days.

I spent lunchtimes in the library where I felt safer. Interacting with adults was easier for me than navigating friendships with kids, and the quiet space helped me regulate.

I stayed physically close to teachers or Mum during stressful moments. Being near a safe adult helped me feel more secure in unfamiliar or overwhelming situations.

Sensory and movement regulation

During this time, I had more help from the speech therapist with swallowing and I was learning to drink liquids without the thickener in them. I was also learning to drink form regular cups, not spouts or lids with only a few holes. That was a big step for me. It helped me feel more normal.

I used sensory fidgets during class. Having something in my hands helped me focus and manage my anxiety as long as I used quiet ones that did not distract others.

I practised deep pressure techniques from my OT. Things like pushing my palms together or sitting with weighted items helped settle my nervous system. She did the Alert program with me and taught me about the Zones of Regulation. My psychiatrist added the purple zone, the catastrophic zone, for me. (https://alertprogram.com/free-resources/)

I had short movement breaks when I needed to reset. Even just getting up, stretching, or walking helped reduce overwhelm and made it easier to return to tasks.

Tools for calming and focus

I used mindfulness strategies when I was calm. Breathing slowly while holding a special object helped me.

I coloured in or did quiet activities when I was overwhelmed. These calming tasks gave my brain and body time to catch up before I could learn.

I held a special object to focus on while breathing. This helped me avoid spiralling into panic and gave me something safe to concentrate on.

I developed my own soft, silent, sensory fidgets to help me as I didn't like noisy, clicky plastic ones. They felt like a therapy pet when I couldn't have a pet with me.

Building emotional safety

Teachers learned to spot my anxiety before it became a meltdown. They didn't wait until I exploded—they acted early, gently, and with care.

I had a secret signal I could use if I needed help. That way, I didn't have to explain everything or feel embarrassed in front of the class.

My needs were explained to the class in a respectful way while I was sent on a message to the library with the aide. It gave the kids a chance to ask questions without me being embarrassed. This helped other kids understand me better and reduced the chance of misunderstandings or teasing. Other kids in the class would look after me on the playground, some asking if I was okay or if I was lost. It was great that I had people who cared.

Working as a team

My psychiatrist, psychologist, OT, Mum, Grandma, and teachers all worked together. They each understood a different part of me, and when they shared ideas, it helped everything feel more consistent. Mum used the information from everyone to create a detailed table of each medical condition, how it affected me and strategies that could help to share with the teachers.

We used the Iceberg Strategy to show what was underneath my behaviour. Instead of seeing just the anger or anxiety, we talked about what was going on inside, like fear, sadness, or overwhelm.

My psychiatrist created a Venn Diagram with 3 circles representing my NVLD, my anxiety and my medical issues. She explained that if any one of those was problematic for me at any time, the other two would be affected. If I was anxious about something, it would make my NVLD symptoms worse and my sympathetic nervous system would be impacted, which would make my medical issues more pronounced. It helped me understand what was happening in my mind and body and why I was in the red or purple zones.

Practising real life through imagination

I used imaginary friends to practise social situations. They helped me work through what to say, what to do, and how things might go. I could try different responses and scenarios that mimicked real life.

I acted out conversations and scenarios in my head. Doing this helped me feel more prepared and less panicked when similar things happened in real life. Unfortunately, sometimes I would be doing this in class, which meant I missed the learning. Not really a good choice, but honestly, sometimes what I was playing in my head was more fun than being in reality and struggling to interpret real people, their facial expression, tone of voice etc.

Writing as a way to cope

Writing my pixie stories helped me make sense of my thoughts. When I didn't know how to talk about something, I could write it down. It helped me process what I was going through but was easier to have a character experience that emotion. It was one step removed from me. It felt like it was happening to someone else, not me.

Sakaela the Sneezy Pixie Visits Amy is about overcoming fears of medical procedures. *Zizzy the Wheezy Pixie Meets Moondrop* talks about the fear of having an asthma attack and going to hospital, but it also brings in fun, magic and inclusion when Zizzy meets a little pixie who has lost his hair from chemotherapy. He is struggling with the unwanted side effects of medicines too. *Minksy the Meltdown Pixie Helps Tommy* is all about dealing with anxiety and using sensory tools to help you feel calm. My stories reflected what was happening for me.

As I got older, I also wrote my feelings in notebooks, sometimes as letters to myself or my Grandpa because I missed him so much.

Unhelpful Strategies

Support that didn't match how I felt

I was told to "take a deep breath" when I was already overwhelmed and I had already flipped my lid. I wasn't in the thinking part of my brain. I needed support to calm down first, then I could focus on deep breathing.

I was told to write my worries and put them in a box. It felt very overwhelming. Once I started listing the worries, I couldn't stop. It was like the little boxes of past trauma and anxiety in my brain all popped open, one after another.

Ignoring important advice

Some teachers ignored advice from my psychiatrist. They were inflexible and they didn't understand my triggers or how my brain worked. The psychiatrist ended up helping me change classes. It was difficult for me because I had to learn to interpret another teachers' social cues. He liked to joke but I wasn't always sure if they were jokes.

Teachers ignored advice from my mother too, who was an experienced special education teacher. Mum knew me best, but when they dismissed her input, I was the one who suffered the consequences.

Too much pressure and work

I was asked to catch up on a full term of schoolwork after being sick throughout the term. It was way too much. I felt like a failure before I had even started. It would have been much more helpful if the teacher had been aware of my incomplete work before the end of term so I could have done the work over time instead of laying it all on me the weekend before the showcase for parents.

I was seated next to the teacher so she could "help" me, but all it did was make me feel threatened and 'watched'.

I was placed next to a bully so we could "work it out." That made me feel unsafe. I was constantly on edge, waiting for something bad to happen. My anxiety was very high, so not surprisingly, my NVLD symptoms were exacerbated as were my medical issues, which just resulted in more absences from school.

Taking away what made me feel safe

My lunch support with the teacher aide was removed. Someone thought I was too reliant on her, but she was the one person I felt safe with. Losing her made everything worse. I started isolating myself even more to stay away form kids with dairy and not be a burden on my friends.

Harmful responses to crisis

I was threatened with expulsion after I had suicidal thoughts caused by medication. I didn't feel supported. I felt like I was being punished for struggling. I told the teacher aide I felt like running away. I wasn't going to run away from school, but I felt like it. I thought she was my safe person to talk to. I didn't expect to be sent to the office, a place I feared, then get suspended for the rest of the week and told to come back after the holidays when the medicine was sorted. That only happened to kids who were really naughty. I didn't understand what I had done wrong.

Even though I had some terrible experiences during these years, I also started to understand myself a little better. I learned that it wasn't my fault that I needed more help. I wasn't being dramatic or naughty: I was trying my best. The people who took the time to listen, support me gently, and include me made all the difference. I still use some of those strategies today. And I hope other kids going through tough times can be given those same chances to feel safe and understood.

28

Strategies for Ages 10–16

From age 10 to 16, life didn't get any easier. In some ways, it waseeven harder. My dad had cancer, my chronic pain started, along with severe period pain, and I had anaphylaxis again. I had to manage medication-induced depression and anxiety. Even though I had stopped the epilepsy medicine, the depression lingered. I was started on fluoxetine, which also had terrible side effects of giving me horrific images so had to be stopped.

After my severe episode of anaphylaxis, I was dealing with PTSD again, and I was diagnosed with OCD as well. Even though some people thought I was "okay" because I could talk well or do certain things, I was struggling a lot on the inside. I felt like I had to hide how I was really feeling. There were days when I didn't even want to be here anymore.

The strategies that helped the most were the ones that gave me hope, distraction, support, or helped me understand what was happening inside my brain. The things that didn't help usually made me feel like a burden or like I wasn't being taken seriously. I needed people to believe me, not just brush it off.

These are the strategies that helped and the ones that didn't from my perspective, but every person is different. I hope some of these will help the young people in your life to boost their self-esteem and help them build resilience to cope with life's challenges.

Helpful Strategies

Understanding my brain and reactions

My psychiatrist took about 6 months to make a book about my life that explained how trauma had affected my brain. It helped me understand that my amygdala was firing because it thought I was in danger, even when I wasn't. Knowing this helped me stop blaming myself for the way I reacted and start seeing it as something that made sense.

Releasing stress through movement

Yoga helped me calm my body and focus my mind. It gave me time to just breathe and stretch and feel more in control of myself.

Aerials gave me a sense of strength and freedom. Hanging, spinning, and climbing helped me feel powerful in a body that often felt weak from pain.

Doing physical exercise of any kind gave me a way to release built-up emotion and tension. It reminded me that I was still capable.

My exercise physiologist helped me participate in rehabilitation at the YMCA gym. I love it. I feel independent when I can ride my bike there by myself because I know the way. I can move and participate in activities he designs especially to help me, and it makes me feel part of the adult world, a place where I am accepted for who I am, where I can laugh and joke. There was also a personal trainer and remedial massage therapist. It has been more beneficial than any psychologist appointments.

Using mindfulness and calming tools

Meditation gave me quiet moments where I could tune in to my body and breath. Even just a few minutes helped me feel more grounded, more connected to this moment instead of worrying about tomorrow.

Listening to white noise helped block out overwhelming background sounds when I was overstimulated.

Hand pan music gave my brain something soft and rhythmic to focus on. It calmed me without needing words or explanation.

I used my own sensory fidgets to help me. I even took my Sensorian in the ambulance with me.

Finding hope in the digital world

Device time helped me more than people realised. It distracted me, but it also gave me a window into the world of other people who were experiencing similar conditions, like me.

Instagram reels, YouTube shorts, and TikToks became a source of comfort for me. Some made me laugh. Some helped me cry. Others gave me hope for the future, which was crucial when I was feeling really distressed.

Following influencers who talked about mental health and body image helped me feel understood. Their stories reminded me that healing was possible.

I have provided details of the ones that helped me in the Breathing and Support section of this book.

Drawing strength from faith and music

Listening to Christian music made me feel connected to something bigger than myself.

Worship songs gave me words when I didn't have my own.

Knowing that God loved me—no matter what—helped me keep going when everything felt too hard.

Listening to positive messages in songs was a really important part of my surviving, so I have listed some of these in the Breathing and Support section too.

Using sensory tools for emotional comfort

Sensory fidgets, especially soft and cuddly ones, were a big comfort during tough times. Just having something squishy to hold or run my fingers over helped regulate my nervous system and gave me something safe to focus on. This is the time when I couldn't find soft, silent, sensory fidgets so I developed my own.

My Cozipals have no eyes so they don't care what you look like. They have ears to hear your worries but no mouth to share your secrets and they live on hugs and snuggles. My Sensorians are a bit more discreet, so I can hide them up my jumper sleeve or put them in my pocket. One of my Sensorians came with me in the ambulance. It was great to be able to fidget quietly when I was scared. My worry beads help me once I calm down a bit, to take ten deep breaths as I slide the beads along the string and my little keyrings are great little finger fidgets that I can hold or hide or attach to pencil cases or bags. It has been great to hear how these simple objects have helped so many people, from little 3-year-olds right up to teenagers and adults.

I am happy that something I make is helping so many other people. Feeling happy is a great way to combat my depression, so it has really helped me. I think making others happy draws your attention away from yourself and puts your focus on others.

Connecting with animals for emotional support

My guinea pigs were like therapy pets. When everything felt heavy, holding them helped. Their soft fur, gentle movements, and little noises brought comfort. They didn't judge or talk. They just let me be, and somehow that helped me feel less alone. the down side of them is when they become sick. One of my guinea pigs died and that was extremely stressful, but as I held him. I also felt him at peace. It gave me a greater understanding of death and dying.

I tried a dog, but that was too stressful, so we had to get rid of it after only a couple of days. I could not handle the unpredictability of a puppy. Sometimes it would be calm and lay down to be patted, but other times it would be jumpy and snappy. Mum had tried to warn me that this would not work, but I didn't believe her. Sometimes we need to try things ourselves to learn from our mistakes. My sister took it and now I can see it when I like, but it is also more settled now it is older.

I participated in some equine therapy. Spending time with horses helped me regulate my emotions and build my confidence. Their calm presence and the gentle rhythm of grooming or walking beside them made a big difference when I was feeling overwhelmed. As long as I had my antihistamines, was covered from head to toe and washed my hands, my allergy to horses was manageable.

Writing as a way to express my emotions

Writing helped me make sense of my thoughts. When I didn't know how to talk about something, I could write it down. It helped me process what I was going through—and sometimes even find meaning in it.

Finding identity through success and creativity

Being an entrepreneur gave me something to be proud of. It helped me see myself as more than just my diagnoses. I was able to see that the work I was doing was helping others. That was very rewarding and gave my life purpose. It helped not only boost my self-esteem, but those feelings of self-worth were helpful when I had suicidal thoughts.

Becoming an author of the *Our Pixie Friends Series* gave me a voice and a way to share my ideas. I was a child speaking to other children in a magical way that helped to 'normalise' some of what we go through. It helped me advocate for others who may be too young to express themselves effectively.

Helping others to find purpose and hope

Supporting others gave me a reason to keep going. It reminded me that even though I felt broken, I could still help someone else feel less alone. Helping others helped me feel useful, not just like a person with problems.

Speaking to others about my journey reminded me that what I had to say mattered. Hearing feedback form audiences about how one little thing I had said made such a difference to them was very empowering. I will never forget some of them. One lady came up to me after I had completed a talk about suicidal ideations called 'From Despair to Hope' (on my 16th birthday!) and what she said will remain in my heart forever. "Thank you so much. I have had suicidal thoughts, and your talk just gave me hope." Wow!

Unhelpful Strategies

Minimising what I was going through

Being told to "just take a deep breath" when I was in panic mode didn't help. It felt like people didn't understand how scared I was, especially after something as serious as anaphylaxis. That kind of advice made me feel like my reactions were wrong instead of valid.

Forcing me to relive trauma without support

Some psychologists kept making me talk about the same traumatic events again and again. Instead of helping me heal, it left me feeling more drained, more stuck, and more broken. I needed support and validation, not to be pushed back into things I had already dealt with.

Overloading me with appointments

Having too many appointments made my life feel like one big problem to fix. I didn't have enough time left for fun, rest, or just being a kid. I needed time to breathe, not just endless plans and programs.

Mum stopped a lot of the appointments and spent that money on doing fun things. Putting joy back into my life was a really valuable step towards healing.

Dismissing or ignoring my voice

When I opened up and people brushed it off, it made me feel invisible. I didn't need them to fix everything. I just needed to be heard and taken seriously. Feeling ignored made me want to shut down and stop asking for help.

Making me feel ashamed for struggling

Being told to "get over it" or "just move on" made me feel like I was weak. It made me ashamed of my feelings and afraid to be honest. Instead of helping, it pushed me to put on my "I'm fine" mask, to pretend I was okay when I wasn't.

Putting adult emotional pressure on me

Some peers, and even adults I met, leaned on me when they weren't coping themselves. They looked to me for emotional support when I was barely holding on. It made me feel like I had to protect them too, and that was too much to carry. It made me want to withdraw more from relationships.

This stage of my life showed me how powerful it is to have the right kind of support. I didn't need people to fix everything. I needed them to walk alongside me, to give me tools, to believe in me, and to see the good in me even when I couldn't see it myself.

When adults gave me a voice, let me rest, reminded me of my strengths, and created safe spaces, it made a difference. And when I found ways to help others, it gave me back a little piece of hope that I thought I'd lost.

I really hope that some of what I have shared helps the kids you care about or work with

Strategies for Neurodiversity

29

I Want to Talk: Social Communication Strategies

Social communication was one of the hardest things for me growing up. These strategies really helped me understand what people meant, how to ask for help, how to express myself, and how to manage in everyday situations.

These strategies were created for NVLD, but they might also help other kids with neurodivergence like autism or ADHD. Everyone is different, so I'm not saying these will work for the child in your life but maybe they could help.

Use social scripts. Use language to talk about events, what happened and why. Create or draw these while you talk to the child so they understand the visual images. Then use these to practise common scenarios, especially how to ask teachers for assistance or what to do in common social situations.

Help the child recognise their own emotions. Visuals may help initially but need to go beyond a smile or frown to include understanding of context and the reasons why they or others feel that way. Using language to explain emotions is very important for children with NVLD as it is their strength.

Teach facial expressions but also include possible alternate meanings. Highlighting how eyes, eyebrows and mouth shapes can express emotions was important for me, but I needed to also learn that it depended on the context to avoid overgeneralisation. For example, eyebrows together in the middle could represent anger or maybe the person is thinking about a puzzling problem, expressing confusion or even squinting in bright sunlight.

Watch television shows or movies together. Pause and rewind streamed movies or shows to identify nonverbal cues that assist with comprehending characters' behaviours. This was great for me. Mum would stop and ask, "What do you think that character is feeling? Why do you think they said that?" Then we would rewind and I could learn to look at another character's eyes or the way they looked at someone so I could understand more fully what was going on. It helped me learn that so much of our communication is nonverbal.

Use language to help the child understand the social context. For kids with NVLD, language is our strength. It's how we understand and process our world. That is not always the case with neurodivergent kids, so find their strength. I found it very helpful talking about a situation I had viewed or read about. Using language to also help me understand social contexts in situ was important. If I was having a problem at the park, Mum might call me over and explain what was going on and how I could handle it. For example, one day I was being very polite and letting other kids go down the slide before me. Mum called me over and explained that it was very kind of me, but I had the right to have a turn too, so I needed to stay in that place and move up in the line.

Explicitly teach about sarcasm and hidden meanings. Teach idioms and be careful not to use them when speaking to the child. E.g., 'Pull your socks up'. *It's Raining Cats and Dogs* by Michael Barton is a great resource for this. It compares literal and inferred meanings for common sayings. You could make your own comic book pages with cartoons for literal meanings on one side of the page, and the cartoon for the actual meaning on the other.

Watch video scenarios of appropriate and inappropriate interactions. Neurodivergent children are often easy targets for kids who don't understand. Being prepared for these situations and knowing how to respond to bullying or teasing can help the child identify the tone of voice and other nonverbal clues. Then help them practise formulating an appropriate response. These scenarios could be turned into social scripts for practice but let the child know they cannot be prepared for every possible scenario. It is important to let the child know that it's okay to get it wrong sometimes as even adults make mistakes.

Use 'shadowing' on the playground. Observe the child unobtrusively when they are playing. If they come across difficulties, watch what they do and intervene if necessary. Don't humiliate them, but call them over and quietly explain what is happening so they can engage more successfully with their peers. Mum would often do this. She would be reading her book so it wasn't obvious to anyone, but if I was having trouble, she would call me over to 'give me a drink' and explain things to me. For instance, she explained that if I kept being polite and letting everyone else go down the slide first, I would never get a turn. It was okay for me to stand my ground and stay in the line.

Be aware of possible literal interpretations of what you say. "No talking" doesn't exclude gesturing, patting someone on the shoulder or mouthing words. Gently correct their understanding without reprimanding if they did not fully understand.

Explicitly teach the impact of tone of voice. 'Great job' can mean you did well or be sarcastic. 'Come here' can be friendly or scolding. Point these out when they come up in situ and explain the context.

These strategies made a big difference to me, and I hope they help others too.

30

Calm During Storms: Regulation Strategies

Emotional regulation and anxiety are things I've struggled with all my life. I often felt overwhelmed, scared, or panicky, sometimes for reasons even I didn't fully understand. These strategies helped me feel safer, more in control, and more supported.

All of these strategies helped to support me with NVLD, but they might help children with other forms of neurodivergence too, like autism or ADHD, or other children struggling with anxiety.

Use a gentle approach. When separating the child from the parent, guardian or other safe, trusted adult, be gentle and kind. The old 'rip the child away and they'll be right when the Mum is gone' attitude couldn't work for me. The child relies on this person to help them navigate the world and interpret people, so they will not cope if they are suddenly without their support person. It took 3 weeks of gradually spending more time in class without Mum before I was able to be left for a whole day. Of course, this is different for every child and depends on previous traumatic events.

Ensure the child meets the teacher for the following year before school ends. In some schools, children are not told about the teacher for the following year until they turn up on the first day. How scary! I would have stressed all holidays about the unknown. This will need to happen every year until the student is quite old, long after the age you would normally stop this practice (even in high school for kids with severe anxiety). Make sure the known, safe teacher is there to introduce the child to the new teacher. The known teacher should stay for a while, not 'drop and go'.

Meet the teacher again before school starts. During the week before school, I would have an appointment to go and meet the teacher again. It was an opportunity to 'break the ice' with them again and familiarise myself with the new classroom, learn routes to toilets, where my bag would go and discuss any fears. It was a very important part of my transitioning from year to year.

Teach the child to recognise their own emotions. A poster of facial expressions or a flip book on a ring may help. Teach the Alert program to help the child learn about zones of regulation – blue zone, green zone, red zone...(https://alertprogram.com/free-resources/)

Teach the hand model of the brain to assist the child to understand the role of the amygdala and what happens when they 'flip their lid'. (Just Google search: Hand Model of the Brain.) You can use this when they do flip their lid to help them calm down first before they can talk about what happened to upset them.

Learn about the Circle of Security and understand that often anxious children need to return to you in order to feel safe. Be open to them returning instead of pushing them away as they need you to help them regulate their emotions. They need you to help them feel safe. (https://www.circleofsecurityinternational.com/pages/what-is-the-circle-of-security)

Teach a range of strategies to help the child calm down using the senses. These are things that help me. I like to listen to handpan or relaxation music and songs with positive messages, chew crunchy foods like carrots or apple or chew gum, read a book, sit in a quiet place especially in nature, move my body using the park equipment so I can hang upside down and I use sensory fidget toys, especially soft, gentle ones which have a more calming effect than noisy, clicky ones. (Our Pixie Friends have Sensorians, Cozipals and worry beads if you require silent fidgets that won't disturb others. Some schools have a Cozipal for the class.)

Teach mindfulness. Mindfulness and meditation strategies help me like yoga or other gentle exercise. Use colouring or art therapy to calm down.

Provide a quiet, safe space. Sometimes there needs to be a quiet, calm, safe place for the child to retreat if they feel overwhelmed. This safe place may be filled with cushions and pillows or other sensory items to create a welcoming, calm environment. A 'cubby' made with sheets over a table can be effective or a little tent if available. (If it is in a school, ensure children are visible to the staff to avoid any chance of misbehaviour, bullying or abuse in there.) At home, there might be a safe place in their room with cuddly items and maybe soft fairy lights.

Physical Touch can help calm. Hugs and cuddles, an arm around the shoulders, pat on the back or holding the child's hand and keeping them close may be appropriate, especially in new or unfamiliar locations or situations. Check with the child, parents and school policies if needed. This will depend on the child's age and past experiences. I needed lots of cuddles and deep pressure to feel safe and loved. Mum knew how important it was for teachers to provide physical and emotional support, so she gave permission. However, a child who has experienced abuse may recoil and become more stressed.

Prepare the child for any changes or new experiences. Keep the child close to you as needed but preparations may help ease the stress. Preparing for new experiences helps us know what is going to happen, especially if they involve going to a different place e.g. a new park, another person's house, a birthday party, new classroom, hall, oval... We read lots of books when I was younger or saw videos online of the new place, so I was less scared of the unknown. Going on a driving holiday was one of my worst experiences. As a kid, Mum had loved driving holidays where the family jumped in the car and headed off, finding where to stay as night fell. For me, that was my worst nightmare. I had no idea where we were going to be, where we would be staying, how long we would be in the car... Mum learnt very quickly that what she had loved was not going to work for me. As soon as we left home, I wanted to go back to my stable environment. Next time we go away, she will show me photos of the place we are staying and use the one location as a base to explore, always coming back at night.

Role play. Playing upcoming events or procedures can help the child be prepared. Role play can also be used after an event to help process what happened and prepare for future occurrences.

Magic can help. Depending on the child's religion and beliefs, magic can help. For example, Magic Pixie Crystals and a special rhyme can help a child feel brave. (These are available from Our Pixie Friends. The book *Sakaela the Sneezy Pixie Visits Amy* explains their use.) I would often write to fairies and tell them how I was feeling or what I was worried about. It was like talking to a friend. Sometimes they would write back. That's why I love it when children e-mail the pixies in Sprizzletania and they write back. One little girl regularly emails us. She has eczema and feels alone in her struggles, so chatting to Our Pixie Friends helps her feel less alone. (Don't worry. All our email communications are checked by a registered teacher and we use the parent's or guardian's email so it is all safe. We can notify the adult if we are concerned about anything the child discusses.)

Read books about overcoming fears and dealing with anxiety. *Sakaela the Sneezy Pixie Visits Amy* is about overcoming fears. *Minksy the Meltdown Pixie Helps Tommy* is about using sensory tools (Minksy's Sprizzletastic Calming Kit and Worry Beads) to help cope with anxiety. *The Kissing Hand* by Audrey Penn can help those 'starting school jitters' and separation anxiety, especially if a laminated handprint of the child is sent home to be kissed (preferably with bright lipstick) by a parent. The hand can be kept on a wall or in the child's locker so during the day if they become distressed, they can be 'kissed' by the parent.

Be kind and understanding. Do not ignore the signs of anxiety such as complaining of fingers or tummy hurting, or headaches. It is important these children know you care so they feel safe. Do not brush the child off.

Use the Iceberg Strategy with the child. What you see may only be the tip of the iceberg. They may have numerous, bigger worries under the surface. Help them identify their worries so they can also learn to get back on track with whatever they need to be doing.

These strategies helped me feel less anxious and more in control. They helped me feel safe, understood, and supported. That makes a huge difference when you're a kid trying to make sense of a scary world. I hope they help the young people in your life too.

31

Help Me: Executive Function Strategies

Executive function, organisation, and planning are some of the hardest things for kids with NVLD. I struggled with this a lot. I found it hard to plan ahead, break down tasks, organise my stuff, and remember what I was meant to do. These difficulties affect me at home and at school. These strategies helped me and might help other kids too, especially if they have NVLD or other neurodivergent needs like ADHD or autism.

Use exemplars, samples and models. We need to see what we are expected to do. Samples show us effectively. Point out what makes one example better than another. Don't assume we will notice the differences.

Create a dictionary of genres or mathematical terms. I had trouble trying to remember terms. What's a polygon or a quadrilateral? What's the difference between an argument and a discussion? Mum helped me create a reference guide with various samples and exemplars showing different standards of work so I could refer to it.

Do not expect generalisation from one subject or lesson to the next. Do not expect the child to be able to generalise the knowledge from one context to another without support. You might easily see the connection to last week's work, but they may not without being told.

Don't confuse the child with multiple frameworks. Teach planning strategies. Keep it simple so they can learn a pattern and use it everywhere. Mum taught me the basic idea of introduction, body with separate points in each paragraph and conclusion. This simple framework is easy for me to remember now that we have practised it over and over and over. It works for my journal articles, essay tasks, talks and even these book chapters.

Practise problem-solving strategies. Keep uncluttered, clear, visual prompts handy. Try to keep the strategies consistent from one year to the next. It was very confusing when different teachers taught me different things. One teacher taught me RUDDS for maths word problems. It was great – read, underline, decide, do, say. I was just getting the hang of it when another teacher taught FISH – find, information, strategy and I can't remember what the H was for. Encourage See, Plan, Do, Check to determine if efforts were successful, even for simple cutting activities.

Use direct instruction. I learn best when I can listen and ask questions as they come to me. Use explicit, direct teaching with step-by-step practice and immediate feedback when learning new material. Allow for questions and clarification at any stage of the explanation rather than making us wait until the end as by then, we can be completely lost and the confusion causes anxiety. Revise concepts in different ways. We can write it, draw it, make a model or answer questions. Some of us need lots of repetition.

Use graphic organisers that are not too cluttered or complex. Make sure any visuals at home or school are easy and uncluttered like simple star charts, tables or Venn diagrams. Model them, create them together and then encourage independence. Children with NVLD may need assistance working out how to use the space on the paper effectively. Layout is difficult without visual-spatial awareness. We might end up putting it all in one little corner, or start at the bottom of the page.

Help children break major tasks into small, manageable parts. Morning and night time routines can be helped by using velcroed visuals on a chart so we can move them from one side to the other as we complete the tasks. Assist with breaking complex tasks into small, sequential parts – do not expect us to be able to do this independently. This goes for school too. Giving us an assignment without scaffolding is setting us up for failure.

Help us with projects and assignments. When doing a research project, teach the sequence of identifying key questions, taking notes on each of those questions, then summarising each section before the actual presentation. Kids with executive function difficulties like me sometimes jump straight to preparing a fancy cover page and miss the important steps. It's not that we can't do the work. We just need help planning what's important and the steps we need to take to complete the whole task.

Provide assistance and scaffolding long past the age independence is usually expected. I still need help or reminders sometimes to go back because I missed the planning stage.

Provide scaffolding for organisation. Assist with packing their bag. These children may have difficulty orienting lunchboxes etc to fit in the space. Items may be strewn around the bag because it is too hard to work out how to fit them inside and even which things should go where. Help us pack our bags, especially getting started. Suggestions like, "Pop your lunchbox down the side." Laptop bags with all materials needed for each subject so kids don't waste time and get stressed gathering all required items is helpful, even if it means doubling up on resources. Coloured folders might help some kids if they are labelled clearly.

Create laminated checklists. Checklists can be used for lessons or items to take for classes that day. These can be ticked off in whiteboard marker and erased for use again next week. This really helps with things like library days, and sports days when special equipment is required. These can also help if the timetable is a rotating timetable with Day 1, 2 etc, although these mixed up days make it very hard for kids with organisational difficulties, so try to keep the same routine as much as possible.

Prepare us for changes to routines. If there are changes to the day, we can go into stress mode. If we were going to the beach but now it's raining, we can have difficulty with that. It's not that we are having a tantrum, but that what is happening doesn't match the plan we thought we had in our mind. If a teacher is away so there is a different class at that time, let us know at the start of the day (or the day before if you know about the change) and help us reorganise what we need and where we need to be. One time of confusion can throw us off for the whole day.

Encourage the use of lists and setting timers as reminders. Some of us have no concept of time so cannot estimate the time it will take to complete tasks. The Teux Deux app may be helpful for older children. Mum taught me how to 'back plan'. We start with the time we need to be somewhere, then list all the things we need to do to get ready, thinking how long they will take. For example, we need to be there by 6 pm. It is an hour's drive, so we need to leave at 5. That means I will need to be having dinner at 4.30. My shower will need to be at 4, so I will need to stop work and bring my guinea pigs inside at 3.30. This helps me a lot. If we didn't do this, I would still be sitting on the couch at 4.55, saying, "It's okay. It doesn't start until 6."

Make homework expectations clear and record them. Help us record homework requirements correctly and in as much detail as possible. We may have heard part of the instruction but tuned out for other parts, so when we get home, it becomes very stressful if we don't know what to do. Ensure we have written it correctly before we leave class.

All of these strategies made life easier for me. They helped me stay more organised and manage the daily tasks that other kids seemed to do without even thinking. I still struggle, especially at home with all my personal care, but that's okay. Nobody is perfect.

32

Look Over Here: Focus and Attention Strategies

Sometimes it's hard to focus, not just because you're distracted, but because you don't fully understand what you're meant to do, or because your brain is busy trying to manage too many things at once. For kids with NVLD, ADHD, or social communication differences, paying attention can be a big challenge. These strategies helped me. Hopefully, they might help other kids too.

Ensure eye contact when giving instructions. It helps us focus and makes it more likely that we're actually taking in what you're saying. If we're not looking at you, we might not even realise you're speaking to us.

Give clear, simple instructions, one or two at a time. Long lists or complicated directions can be overwhelming. It's easier for us to follow steps when they're broken down clearly.

Be aware of literal interpretations of what you say. If you say, "Rule a line at the top of your page," and you actually mean "Rule a line along the top blue line," we might do something completely different. Say exactly what you mean.

Ask the student to repeat the instructions in their own words. This helps check that we've understood properly and haven't tuned out or misinterpreted what you said. Playing auditory sequential memory games can be fun and help us pay attention. Mum used to say things like, "Walk to the fridge, tap it 3 times, then jump around the table twice and skip back here." She started with just 2 instructions and built it up over time. I had to focus because if I didn't, I'd have to start all over again until I got it right and experienced success. It was great fun.

Ensure the task is at the right level. If it's too hard, we might give up or get frustrated. If it's too easy, we might zone out. Getting the balance right helps us stay engaged.

Use sensory fidgets if they help that child and don't distract others. For some of us, fidgeting actually increases our focus. Wobble cushions, stretchy toys, weighted lap blankets or textured items can make a big difference.

Incorporate short, frequent movement breaks. These breaks help reset our attention. Pixie Challenge Cards or fun little movement prompts are great for younger kids and can help us refocus. Sometimes just the act of walking away and bouncing a ball five times is enough to reset and aid attention. There are lots of other brain break ideas online.

Consider where we're seated. Try to avoid places with too many distractions, like near windows, tv's, doors, or noisy classmates or the road with constant traffic. The less visual and auditory chaos, the easier it is to concentrate. Minimise distractions like PA announcements. Sudden loud noises or interruptions can pull our attention away and it's hard to get it back. Noise-cancelling headphones or headphones playing study music can be helpful to remove other distractions.

Give positive praise for attending and following through on tasks. Even if it's something small, it builds our confidence and helps us feel like we're capable.

Don't shame or embarrass us for asking questions. We might have missed what you said or only caught a few words. Saying things like, "Weren't you listening?" makes us feel small and scared to speak up again. **Be prepared to explain things again and again in multiple ways.** Sometimes we need to hear it differently for it to make sense, especially if we're feeling anxious or overloaded. At these times, it is even harder to pay attention.

Provide plenty of opportunities to ask questions and answer them respectfully. Let us know that it's okay to be unsure. We'll be more likely to engage if we know we won't be judged.

Use multiple senses to help with understanding and attention. Visuals, pointing, gestures, and sound cues can help lock the instruction into our brains more clearly than just spoken words.

Be aware of group tasks. These can be extra tricky when there's lots of talking and movement. We might need check-ins or reminders to help us stay focused and understand our role.

Sometimes we need help getting started, staying on task, or finishing the work. Gentle, private reminders work best. A soft voice, a light touch on the shoulder, or a kind question like, "Do you need some help?" can bring us back without making us feel embarrassed. When cleaning a bedroom, it helps to have prompts like, "Maybe start by collecting all the dirty washing on the floor" rather than, "Haven't you finished yet?"

These small changes helped me feel more confident and made it easier to focus and get things done. When the adults around me understood how my brain worked, everything became just a little less overwhelming.

33

Jam Roll: Sensory and Motor Planning Strategies

Sensory and motor difficulties were a big part of life for me growing up. It wasn't just about loud sounds or scratchy clothes. It was about handwriting, coordination, textures, and even how to use scissors or climb a ladder. Kids with NVLD often need extra help with these things. These strategies made things easier for me and might help others too.

Play 'Jam Roll' or "Sausage Roll". Deep pressure activities can help when we're overwhelmed. Wrap us up in a blanket and pretend to spread butter and jam on us (or sauce), applying firm, calming pressure down our back and legs, then playfully pretend to eat us. Adding humour helps break the meltdown cycle.

Provide modified equipment as necessary. Things like spring-loaded scissors, dual control scissors, pencil grips, grip balls, air cushions, and balance boards made tasks more manageable for me and can support others too.

Be careful to choose an appropriate pencil grip. Simple triangular ones worked best for me. Contoured grips were too tricky. I couldn't work out how to place my fingers on it correctly, or which way it was supposed to on my pencil. Be prepared with lots of grips. It takes time to switch them between all the different pencils we might be using, so it is much easier to have one on each pencil.

Assist with motor planning by using language. Ask things like, "Where do you think you need to put your hand to get up that ladder?" Use planning ideas like see, plan, do, check. "Did that work? What else could you try?" This helps us build our thinking and confidence.

Occupational therapy was key for me. It wasn't a quick fix. I did OT for 10 years. Be prepared for the long haul and know that it really can help.

Use explicit verbal instructions and demonstrations for new skills. We might not pick things up by watching others. Clear step-by-step guidance makes a huge difference.

Give positive praise for efforts, not just achievement. Trying matters. Celebrate the little wins and the hard work, even if it's not perfect.

Use handwriting instruction with lots of repetition. Changing line types every year was exhausting. I had to relearn where letters went every time. It would've helped if we just used blue lines and gradually made the spacing smaller. That way, I could focus on what I was writing instead of how to place each letter.

Allow blank paper when you want the focus to be on content. Sometimes the lines are more confusing than helpful, especially when we're still learning how to space our words.

Reduce the amount of handwriting expected. Give worksheets or write some parts for us. Taking photos of the board can also help us keep up without having to copy everything.

Try keyboarding skills or voice-to-text software if handwriting is too hard. Depending on how much trouble we are having, typing or speaking our answers can give us another way to succeed. Chat GPT can transcribe our speech word for word, which allows us to focus on the content of what we want to write rather than stress about the physical act of writing and staying in the lines.

Use sensory fidgets if they help. These tools can help us to focus and stay calm, especially during tasks that are tricky or stressful. Having a fidget in a pocket enables us to have it with us when we need it. The sensory fidgets that I developed are quiet so they don't distract me from my thinking or annoy anyone else. To me that is important. I cannot stand hard, clicky fidgets.

Be aware of sensory overload. Too many visuals, too much noise, bright lights, or even temperature can make it really hard to concentrate or stay calm.

Offer sensory fun tailored to the child. Things like water, playdough, paint, gel beads, or magic sand can be fun and helpful. Hiding little objects in slime or sand can turn it into a game. Just be aware that some kids get stressed with certain textures.

Create obstacle courses to develop memory and motor planning. Use ramps, bridges, tunnels, or stepping stones. Add variety and story elements like "Watch out for crocodiles!" to make it fun and imaginative while building skills.

Pixie Challenge Cards can help with movement breaks and auditory sequential memory. They're quick, playful, and can inspire other creative movements too. I developed these as a kid and used them with my nephews. We all loved them. I would often use them when I was doing homework or homeschooling to give my brain a chance to reset and help me focus on the next task.

Do activities that use both sides of the body. Things like jumping with both feet or using both hands to pull on a scooter board helped me develop coordination and bilateral integration (getting both sides of my brain working together).

Model movements while sitting in front of the child. Start simple, like lifting a hand and placing it on your knee, repeating it five times. As the child gains skill, build up to more complex, repetitive movement patterns using both sides of the body. Marga Grey, my first OT, developed a great program called Coordikids, which helps with a lot of these type activities. (https://www.coordikids.com/consultations/marga-grey/)

These strategies helped make everyday tasks feel a little more possible. They gave me ways to move, play, and learn without becoming overwhelmed, and they helped me build skills at my own pace.

34

Navigating the World: Visual-Spatial Strategies

Visual–spatial skills were one of my biggest challenges. I often got lost, couldn't judge distances, had trouble with handwriting, and didn't know how to lay out my work or use diagrams properly. It affected almost everything I did. For kids with NVLD, these kinds of difficulties can impact schoolwork, safety, sports, and everyday routines. These are the strategies that helped me, and they might help others too.

Teachers are educated about more well-known learning disabilities like dyslexia, but visual-spatial skills are not something they are trained in, which made school so much harder. One of my goals is to highlight the impact of NVLD, and advocate for greater awareness of this condition since it affects millions of people worldwide.

Use language to assist with navigating the environment. Instead of expecting us to find our way on our own, talk us through the route and point out landmarks. Say things like, "Turn left at the red fence," or "Walk past the drinking fountain, then the blue bin." These landmarks become memory hooks that help us feel less lost, but we need the language component to help us navigate.

Never expect the child to navigate complex routes alone. We have no internal map. We might learn one specific way to get somewhere, like from the classroom to the library, but that doesn't mean we can figure it out from a different spot like the oval. A small change in the path can completely confuse us, even if we have been to the destination before. Don't assume we realise that we are just near a familiar building. We may have no idea as we are seeing it from a different angle. I couldn't recognise my own house when I saw it from the neighbour's door. It was a completely different perspective.

Be safety aware in all environments. It can be dangerous if we're expected to cross roads without help, navigate busy campsites, or take part in activities like canoeing or swimming. If we fall out of a canoe, we might not even know which way is up. We need adults to be extra careful and not assume we'll "figure it out." When I was younger, I couldn't even work out how to stand up in a pool. I would be lying horizontally under the water in a wading pool for kids, looking up at Mum, and desperately thrusting my feet 'down', which was actually just straightening my legs. I could not work out how to flip over and put my feet on the bottom of the pool.

Provide assistance and scaffolding long past the age independence is usually expected. Just because we're in high school doesn't mean we can suddenly do things on our own. I still needed help navigating car parks, finding rooms, crossing roads (especially ones with slip lanes when I can't work out which direction the cars are going), figuring out how to set out work on a poster.

These things don't become automatic with age. I will always need support navigating the world.

Offer handwriting instruction using consistent, clear guidelines. One of the hardest parts for me was the constant change in handwriting lines every year. We went from big spaced blue lines to red and blue lines with a dotted line, then to red and blue lines without the dotted line, and eventually back to just blue lines. Every time the lines changed, I had to relearn where to place the letters. It took so much focus just to get the letters to sit right that I couldn't concentrate on what I was actually trying to write. It would make so much more sense if kids just used blue lines from the beginning and gradually made the space smaller over time.

Use AI to help. For some children, voice-to-text software can be a life-changer, especially now that tools like ChatGPT can record our voices and transcribe them word for word.

Use unlined paper for creative writing or thinking tasks. When the focus is on ideas and content, not neatness or handwriting, it is better to remove the stress of keeping the letters between the lines. Blank paper gives us the freedom to just think and express ourselves.

Use language to describe and explain all visual imagery. Picture clues in worksheets, books, or posters are often confusing for us. We tend to zoom in on tiny details and completely miss the big idea. Talking us through what we are seeing and explaining what it means helps a lot. Advertisements and cartoons can be hard for us to understand as we need to interpret all the nonverbal clues.

Provide concrete, hands-on materials for maths concepts, even in older years. Don't assume we have outgrown the need for blocks or counters. We cannot visualise number lines or 'see' quantities in our heads. Without something to touch and move, the ideas don't make sense. I cannot estimate where halfway is along a line. I need to get a piece of string and fold it in half. Using number lines for fractions or positive and negative numbers is really hard for me. I need to see and touch to understand.

Don't ask us to visualise things in our mind. We can't picture a whiteboard or imagine a hundreds board. We don't "see" images when we read or hear descriptions. Estimating halfway across a line or how full a cup is can be impossible. Visualisation doesn't come naturally, and instructions like "picture this in your head" aren't helpful.

Reduce the amount of work that needs to be copied from books or screens. Copying drains our mental energy. Provide worksheets or write some of the task for us so we can focus on understanding instead of just copying. It makes a huge difference. It takes so long to look up and back, searching each time for where we were up to by starting at the top each time. Other kids can estimate they were about half way down the right side of the book, but we have no idea, so we start scanning from the top left page every single time.

Taking photos of smartboards can help. When there are diagrams or detailed notes, a photo means we can go back and look without the stress of rushing to copy everything down correctly.

Keep all learning materials uncluttered. Worksheets and screens should have lots of white space and a clear, logical flow straight down the page. Avoid putting parts of the activity inside boxes or inserting things in random spots. We need simplicity to stay on track.

Be aware of sports safety. In games like netball, we might not understand which areas we're allowed in or where to go. We also have trouble tracking the ball, judging where bats and sticks will land, or understanding the direction of play. It can be dangerous for us and the other kids if we're not supported properly.

Bike riding and road safety need extra attention. We can't always judge how far away cars, curbs, or other bikes are. This puts us, and others, at risk if we're not supported to navigate these spaces safely.

Know that we might hurt others accidentally. If we think we can fit in a small space, but can't, we might bump into someone or knock things over without meaning to. It's not rudeness. It's a lack of accurate spatial awareness.

Help with construction or collage work. Even basic things like where to place sticky tape or glue to hold something together can be confusing. A little help and a lot of patience go a long way.

Support cutting activities by giving clear guidance. Drawing a thick black line from the edge of the paper to the shape we need to cut can help us know where to start. Otherwise, we might freeze or start in the wrong place and ruin the whole task. One time, the OT asked me to cut out a square from a collection of shapes on the page. I had no idea where to start, so I kept turning the page and trying but couldn't find how to get into the square so I ended up just cutting one corner of the paper. Another time, I was helping Mum wrap presents, but when I pulled the paper out from the roll, and then cut the already cut end. I wondered why it didn't work when I had a 1cm wide strip of appear in my hand. See, plan, do, check. Make a new plan.

Don't expect Lego or jigsaws to be at our age level. These are very visual–spatial tasks. For children with NVLD, they may be years behind their chronological age in these areas. That doesn't mean we're not smart. It just means this isn't our strength. I have only been able to do Lego designed for 8+ in the last few years, and sometimes I still need help. Watch our self-esteem when we feel inadequate as much younger kids can do things we can't. It was very hard watching my 6-year-old nephew doing what I still couldn't do when I was twelve.

Always provide visual–spatial tasks at our developmental level, not our chronological age. I was in Year 6 before I could do construction copying tasks usually given to Prep and Year 1 students. I still learned. It just took me longer and I needed the right support. I remember it took me almost a whole day to complete a mosaic task designed for Prep kids when I was in Year 6 or 7. I became very frustrated, but I persevered and eventually got it. I was so proud of myself. That is why homeschooling can be the best option for some kids. It enables us to work at our own pace and feel proud of our achievements without being compared to others or judged by them.

Be aware of the emotional toll these difficulties can cause. When something is hard every day, it chips away at your self-esteem. Offer lots of reassurance and encouragement. Remind us we're not stupid. We just learn differently.

All of these things helped me feel a little more confident and kept me safe. Visual-spatial skills will never come naturally to me, but the right support makes everyday tasks feel more manageable. When adults understand what I need, the world feels a little less overwhelming. We need safe adults who can build us up in a world that constantly seems to want to tear us down.

35

Learning Differently: Academic Strategies

Maths and abstract thinking were really hard for me. I couldn't just picture shapes or numbers in my mind. I didn't know how to spot patterns, solve similar problems, or follow complex instructions. For kids with NVLD, these kinds of tasks can feel confusing and frustrating. Because we often have a high IQ, we know we're capable of understanding things, but it just doesn't click the way it seems to for everyone else. It makes us feel "dumb," even when we're not. These strategies helped take some of the pressure off and made it possible for me to learn and show what I knew, just in a different way than most kids.

Use concrete representations whenever possible. This is especially important when learning concepts like symmetry, rotations, translations, and reflections. We can't "see" shapes or flip things around in our head, even as teenagers or adults. Showing us with blocks, counters, or paper cut-outs helps make these ideas real and less confusing.

Create block designs when needed instead of expecting us to visualise them. If you ask us to calculate the number of edges on a shape we can't see in our mind, we're stuck. Let us build it first, then count it. That's how we learn.

Don't expect us to copy complex diagrams without support. Diagrams are hard to recreate and even harder to place on a page properly. Whenever possible, give us the diagram or create it slowly together, step-by-step. Use clear instructions about where to start and how to fit it on the page.

Be prepared for ongoing difficulty with fractions, place value, measurement, geometry, and algebra. These don't just click into place. I needed concrete examples for a long time—way past the age most people expect. Place value was especially hard. I'd forget it again and again, even after learning it the year before. What helped was repeating it in different ways: drawing place value houses, chalking on the concrete using the crack as the decimal point, using stones for the decimal point and painting with water to build the place value chart on the path at the park, drawing it in books, on whiteboards, on charts. Every year until about Year 7, I had to re-learn it again. That's just how my brain works.

Number lines were almost impossible. They were confusing because they could mean anything—0 to 10, 0 to 10,000, -35 to +35, or even fractions between 0 and 1. You might think you can estimate where halfway or one-third is, but if you can't visualise it and you don't physically fold the paper, you're just guessing. And for me, guessing made me anxious.

Allow extra time to complete tasks or reduce the number of problems on the page. Worksheets with five columns of sums were way too much. It was overwhelming and hard to know where to start. Just two columns was much more manageable and made it possible to think clearly.

Give plenty of space for answers on the same page as the questions. Don't expect us to flick back and forth between books or worksheets. Every time I had to look back at a question, I had to scan the whole page to find my place again. Finding answers in the back of a textbook could take me half an hour. It wasn't because I didn't understand the maths: it's because scanning and searching was exhausting and confusing.

Don't expect us to recognise patterns or apply the same method from one question to the next. I couldn't generalise what I'd learned. Each question looked completely different to me. I needed reminding every time, even when it was technically the same kind of problem.

Be careful with what you say because we might take things literally or overgeneralise. One time, someone told me not to worry about the 0 at the end of a decimal. So when I wrote the number 120, I thought the 0 didn't matter and wrote 12 instead. You might think that's silly, but that's how literal thinking works.

Create a folder of examples and key concepts for us to refer to. A reference guide with worked examples helped me remember what to do when I forgot. It's a great way to reduce panic and help us feel independent.

Teach us how to identify key words in questions. We don't always understand what a question is asking. For example, if you tell us to "use these four websites to find the information," we might think we have to find the same information on *all four* sites instead of just choosing one. Be clear and check that we understand.

Check our inferential comprehension and support us if needed. Sometimes we do not understand what the question is really asking because we do not pick up on implied meanings or have difficulty working out the relevant and irrelevant material. If we struggle to interpret nonverbal cues in social situations in real life, it is even harder to pick up on those cues in the written word. "Follow me" in a text could be interpreted as someone being nice and asking the character to follow or it might be someone with more sinister intentions.

Explicitly teach us how to take notes, and always assist. We struggle to tell the difference between important and unimportant information. That means we might write everything, or we might write nothing at all, just because we don't know what's relevant.

Make sure homework tasks are clearly recorded. Don't assume we'll remember them when we get home. Even if we understood it in class, it might be completely gone from our memory by the time we sit down to do it.

Don't assume we lack the intelligence to do the work. We often have deep thoughts and unique insights. But we need support to show what we know. It's not about ability: it's about how the information is presented and how the task is structured.

Don't rush us. Being timed adds pressure and makes it even harder to do our best. It takes us longer to work out where to write the answer, what steps to take, and how to interpret the layout. One specialist told my mum, "She can do it. She's just working so much harder than everyone else to do the same thing." That stuck with me. It's not about being lazy or slow. It's just more effort for my brain to do what others find easy.

These strategies helped take some of the pressure off. They gave me the chance to learn, think, and show what I knew in a way that worked for me. I might not learn the same way as everyone else, but with the right support, I can still achieve great things.

SECTION FIVE

Additional Material and Resources

36

When God Was the Only Light Left

I know Christianity isn't for everyone, so feel free to skip this chapter if you want to. I'm not here to tell you what to believe or to preach at you. I just want to share how my faith helped me survive some of the hardest moments in my life, because for me, when everything else felt like it was falling apart, God was the only light that didn't go out.

There were times when the world felt really dark, not just outside, but inside me too. I felt weighed down, tired, empty and alone. I didn't always have the words for it, but I felt like I was drowning in sadness or stress or fear. Sometimes, even when I was surrounded by people, I still felt totally alone, like no one could truly see what I was going through.

But God did.

When I had no one else to talk to, I could talk to Him. When I felt like no one understood me, I believed that He did. I didn't have to explain every detail or find the right words. I could just say, "Help," or even nothing at all. He was still there. I didn't need a church building. I didn't need to dress up or get everything perfect. I just needed to be me, wherever I was.

When I was scrolling on social media or watching YouTube, I'd randomly come across Christian influencers saying things like, "If you're seeing this, this is for you," and then they'd pray for anxiety, or mental health, or people who feel broken, and I'd just sit there and cry because it felt like it *was* for me. It was as if God knew I needed that exact message in that exact moment, and He found a way to get it to me.

Other times, I'd turn on the Christian radio station on Google Home or play worship music on my phone, and the lyrics would speak straight to my heart. It was like the songs were written for me, as if someone knew exactly what I was going through and put it into words when I couldn't. The music gave me peace. It reminded me that I was still loved, still seen, still worth something.

There were days when I felt totally broken—when I couldn't stop crying or I just felt so low that I didn't even want to move, but then I'd turn on worship music. I wouldn't even plan it. It just sort of happened. I'd start listening, then I'd hum along, and before I knew it, I was up. I was dancing around my room at midnight in my pyjamas, singing at the top of my lungs, laughing through the tears. That kind of joy doesn't come from nowhere. That's the kind of joy that comes from God. It's not fake or forced. It's real. It reminded me that even when things were tough, there could still be light. There could still be moments of pure, silly, healing joy.

Worship doesn't always look like what people think it does. It's not just church and hymns and prayers. For me, worship is playing a song that lifts my soul. It's whispering a prayer while curled up in bed. It's hearing someone say, "You're not alone," and knowing deep down that God made sure I heard that message.

Christian artists on YouTube also talk openly about their struggles, anxiety, self-worth, fear, pain, and loss. When they share their stories, it helps me feel less ashamed of mine. They show that faith doesn't make everything perfect, but it gives you strength to get through the hard stuff. It gives you hope to keep going. Their songs and their stories remind me that healing is possible, that joy is still allowed, and that God works even in the middle of the mess.

Even if no one else was awake or around, God was there. Even if I didn't say anything out loud, He heard me. And I think that's what helped the most: the fact that I didn't have to be perfect or strong or even "okay." I could just be me, and that was enough for Him.

So yeah, this chapter isn't about religion or rules. It's just me saying that in a world that often felt too loud, too harsh, or too empty, God was a safe place. A light that stayed. A presence I could turn to when no one else understood. A reason to keep dancing, even after crying.

(If you want to know more about the artists who helped me, there are more details in the next chapter about breathing and support.)

37

Breathing and Support

Here are some ideas for support if you need it. They are not a definitive list, just some strategies that may help you because they helped me. Please pick and choose from the lists below. Remember, you are not alone. Your life matters. You are enough just as you are.

If you are struggling, seek professional advice from qualified medical practitioners.

Calming Tools

Handpan music – I like Konstantin Rossler and Malte Marten.

Tibetan bowls – I like Aurabowls.

Frequencies – Just search *anxiety relief frequency* or *chronic pain relief frequency*. The frequencies are so relaxing.

Stacked breaths – Breathe in for as long as you need. Then hold it for as long as you need. Then do a small "top-up" breath (like a sniff), and finally breathe out for as long as feels comfortable. Search *breathing techniques* for other ideas.

Instagram / TikTok / YouTube Accounts

Please note: Most creators listed here are on multiple platforms, so search for them wherever you or your client accesses content (Instagram, YouTube, TikTok, etc.)

MollyCarlson1 – High diver; body image, eating disorders, and anxiety

Ella Nutella Recovers – ED and body image

Youranxietyislying2yew – Mental health, suicide, divorced parents (favourite creator)

DadHowDoI – "Instagram dad" who shows you how to fix things, gives dad jokes, etc. for those who didn't have a dad to show them

BreeLenehan – Body image

Jb_copeland – Mental health and personal growth

Ickes.edward – Mental health

Maarten_ov – Mental health

Nicholasjohn__ – Mental health quotes

Ashleymaland – Domestic violence and SA survivor; quotes

Dancinginthemess – Somatic healing and resilience

Tanyasangani – Interviews people on the street about mental health and personal growth

Michael.galyon – Mindfulness

Annakristinam – Mental health, queer identity, blended family – The "crash out" video with her partner felt like a big warm hug

Humphry The Butler (Angus Villeirs – Stuart) – Dresses as a butler and tackles hard topics like body dysmorphia, anxiety, coming out (LGBTQ+), and mental health in a comforting way

Lucas Jones – Poet and actor, focused on mental health

Jak Piggott – Growth and mental health, especially for boys (but teen girls watch him)

Melissa Romano – Nervous system and healing

Kyle Fuller – Mental health, self-esteem, and worth

Avi Gill – Mental health and self-esteem

Kelsey Brennan – Fitness coach; body image and food guilt

Olivia Lutfullah – ADHD

Jemma Bella – Chronic illness and invisible conditions

Faith Ashenden – Neurohacking, chronic illness, anxiety, and nervous system

Communities for specific needs – e.g. Autism QLD, Dysautonomia community, The NVLD Project

Dr Ryan Worley – Brain rehab specialist

Ali Miles – Sports dietitian for teen athletes

Graciebarrajiujitsu – Self-defence; helps build confidence in keeping yourself safe

Psychbykat – Performance psychology, mental health, and mindset

this.is.the.illness.m.e – Chronic illness advocate

Jake Goodman MD – "I'm a doctor and I take medicine for my mental health."

<u>**Singers / Songs That Helped Me**</u>

Alex Warren (trauma survivor):

Save You a Seat – Grief and loss

Ordinary – Love and realising even traumatised people can be loved

Jared Benjamin – *Beauty In The Hurting* – Chronic pain, being unseen in the medical system

Lewis Capaldi:

Survive – Living through the hard

Love The Hell Out Of You – A reminder that people will love and care about you

Kelly Clarkson:

Broken and Beautiful

Stronger – You are stronger than you think and beautiful as you are

Danny Gokey – Many songs including *Only for a Moment* – Hope in hard times

for KING & COUNTRY – All songs! Mental health, Christian messages

Priceless – A woman's worth after mistreatment

God Only Knows - Nobody else understands what you have been through

Unspoken – *Help is On the Way* – Mental health and knowing people care

Alessia Cara – *Scars to Your Beautiful* – Mental health, self-esteem, body image

SVRCINA – Many songs including *Loyal* – For people who've had their trust broken

James Blunt – *Monsters* – Grief from losing a father

Jessica Baio – *Someday* – Grief from losing a father

Lily Meola – *Butterfly* – Grief from losing a mother

Dean Lewis – *How Do I Say Goodbye* – Cancer and loss

Cimorelli – Many songs around mental health, Christian themes, self-esteem

You're Worth It

I Am Enough

Matthew West – Many songs including *Truth Be Told* – Speaking up when you're not okay

We Are Messengers – *Image of God*

Bella Lambert – *Just 14* – About not having to do everything

Extra Support

000

Lifeline

Groundwire

Beyond Blue and their online forum

MensLine Australia

1800RESPECT

Men's Referral Service

Kids Helpline

Elder Abuse Helpline

Financial Counselling Australia

13 YARN

DV Connect

Ask Izzy – Disability advocacy finder tool

1300 MH CALL

Community centres near you

38

From Idea to Impact – Our Pixie Friends

When I was 6, I was on my way to yet another medical appointment. I was complaining to mum in the back of the car. "Why am I the only one going to these appointments? What's wrong with me? Why am I not 'normal' like the other kids?" Mum, being the kind, caring mother she was said, "Oh suck it up princess, you're not the only one. There are thousands of kids with a lot more to deal with than you." Right then, I decided I wanted to start a business to help other kids feel happy with who they are, feel less alone, and encourage other kids to be kind and inclusive. That was when the idea for Our Pixie Friends was born.

I created my first business plan on the way to and from that appointment. I wanted a website, books, merchandise to sell so I could raise money for medical research and the list went on. Despite some people trying to stop me, I persevered. Four years later, when I was 10, I registered my business officially thanks to a kind, generous lady named Sharron Pountney from SLP Consulting. Now there are many facets to my business. Here is a snapshot of what I do.

1. Merchandise and Sensory Tools

My books link directly to products that support kids' mental health. For example, *Minsky the Meltdown Pixie Helps Tommy* comes with calming kits and worry beads. When a child reads the book, they can also receive the tools the characters use.

I've created a line of soft, silent, wearable sensory tools like fidgets and breathing beads that kids, teens, and adults can use. They're discreet, calming, and designed to reduce anxiety at school or in public.

We now have a full range of sensory keychains, worry beads, and even friendship group kits. Everything I make connects to my mission: to help kids feel less alone and more empowered.

2. Speaking and Workshops

I'm an international speaker and advocate for mental health, trauma, and neurodivergence. Through keynote presentations, school talks, pixie visits, book readings and creative writing workshops, I've shared my lived experience with over 5,000 children, 1,300 teenagers, and 1,700 adults.

My talks in primary and secondary schools focus on helping young people embrace their stories and understand that they're not alone. I speak on topics like overcoming challenges, mental health strategies, kindness, creativity, and entrepreneurship. I also teach writing workshops that inspire kids to turn their stories into books. I encourage young people who are facing challenges to dream and work towards achieve their goals, not letting their challenges stop them.

A highlight is my upcoming plenary session in August at the International Childhood Trauma Foundation Conference in Melbourne where I'll speak to around 3,000 professionals about my journey through trauma, neurodivergence, and hope.

I will also be doing a workshop for 200 people which delves deeper into my neurodiveregence and trauma with some strategies that helped me.

I always work with the person asking me to speak to ensure my presentation meets the goals they are trying to achieve. If you are looking for a speaker for your workplace, conference, school or university, please get in touch.

3. Children's Picture Books

I have published three children's picture books and have a fourth one on the way. My books explore themes like resilience, kindness, and courage, and they're packed with colourful illustrations by a wonderful teen illustrator, Chloe Johnson. and practical tools like calming strategies and worry beads.

My books help kids feel seen, safe, and understood using pixie characters, each with their own medical journeys and friendship struggles, to help children realise they're not alone.

The first book I ever wrote, *Sakaela the Sneezy Pixie Visits Amy*, was written when I was just six years old. I didn't like using my nasal spray, or doing other medical procedures, so I wrote a story to help other kids feel brave too.

My books promote cultivating a kindness culture and it is my hope that kids read my books and develop a greater understanding of their friends, family and those around them.

3. Donations to Medical Research

I donate 10% of all product sales to medical research. I may not be a scientist, but I believe in funding research that could change kids' lives.

By age 13, I had donated $1,500 to support medical research. I've also donated $500 to JDRF (Juvenile Diabetes Research Foundation) and $2,500 to the Institute for Molecular Bioscience at UQ, which studies ways to help babies in the womb with conditions like cancer using zebrafish.

4. Pixie Visits

One of my favourite things is doing Pixie Visits — dressing up and visiting children experiencing trauma or medical needs. I meet kids in hospitals, homes, and at community events to help them feel supported and not so alone.

I bring stickers, stories, and sensory toys — and a whole lot of magic.

5. The Cozipal Project

The Cozipal Project is all about giving gift packs to children experiencing trauma. Each pack includes a picture book, a sensory toy, and a message of hope.

We've already delivered over 500 Cozipal packs, helping kids feel comforted and valued during tough times. I love seeing the smiles on kids' faces when they receive a gift that is just for them. I love showing them that they are cared about beyond measure.

6. Interactive Website

Our Pixie Friends has a fun, interactive website where kids can explore a magical map of where all the pixies live. They can click around, meet each character, and learn about different medical needs in a playful and safe way.

Kids can even upload their own stories and artwork — anonymously and safely moderated — to feel seen and express themselves.

I am passionate about helping young people so if there is anything I can do to help the young people you work with, please let me know by emailing *ourpixiefriends@gmail.com* or check out my website *www.ourpixiefriends.com*.

Final Words

When I was six, I had a dream to raise $1 million for medical research. My donations so far have gone towards vital research into childhood brain cancer and diabetes. Thank you very much for buying this book. 10% of this sale will be donated, so just by reading this book, you have helped a child somewhere.

I hope you have found my insights helpful. In this book, I have shared strategies that helped me, but I am always learning. If you have tried another strategy that has worked well for you, or the young people in your life, I would love to learn it too. If you have any feedback or suggestions, or would like to book me to speak, please contact me or my team.

Have a sprizzletastic day!

Siobhan

Founder/Owner/CEO

Our Pixie Friends Pty Ltd

www.ourpixiefriends.com

ourpixiefriends@gmail.com

(+61) 466 699 700

Acknowledgements

This book would not have happened without the support of many people in my life. I would like to thank:

God – for loving me, being the light in my life, and for giving me the incredible opportunity to help others.

Mum – for believing in me when no one else did. For being my teacher. For being the original Pixie Friend and my proofreader on my many chapter attempts! Thank you for bringing me into this world to help kids. Thank you for supporting my mission. I love you. (And yes, I am aware they were mostly simple sentences!)

Grandma – for staying faithful, showing me what it was like to live a God-filled life. Thank you for supporting me financially and mentally. Thank you for supporting Mum and me to do the work we do and for always loving me no matter what.

My incredible sister, Elise and her wonderful partner, Darian - for supporting us during our lowest time and being there for us throughout the years.

My nephews, Tyler, Lincoln, Aston and Hugo - for bringing me joy and companionship.

My amazing siblings James, Sam and Tamara – for being supportive and cheering on my dreams.

All my incredible friends – for loving and supporting me to be me. Thank you for looking our for me and for all our laughter. I enjoy our times together.

Physical Health and Medical Support

Dr Tim Donovan – for being patient and putting the care into my health. You were there when I needed you at all hours of the night and day. Without you, I wouldn't be here to tell the story. Thank you for my life.

Dr Andrew Ganter, Dr Matthew Harvey, and the team at Sunstate Family Practice – for being patient and understanding and helping me to erase my phobia of doctors.

Dr Richard Muir, Dr David Winkle, Professor Jenny Batch and Dr Julie Beak - for supporting me for years through my personal physical struggles.

Dr Jane Peake and the staff at the Queensland Children's Hospital – for helping me to feel more confident in my care.

All the paramedics at QAS who have saved my life countless times – especially the ones from the Mt Gravatt Station.

Pam Reed, Marga Grey and Marguerite Moir - for helping me understand my world.

Adam Russell – for seeing and supporting me through my complex pain and being okay with changing exercises if they hurt or don't feel 'right'. Thank you for never making me feel silly for having pain. Thank you for not making me feel like the pain was all in my head.

Kaine Doblo – for bringing humour into my pain journey, explaining exercises the way I would understand with my neurodivergence, and for never making me feel upset that I have pain.

Shane Weigman – for being so understanding of my pain and supporting me to feel more in control of my pain and body. Thank you for answering all my questions and for never making me feel weird for needing help.

The Pain Clinic team at Queensland Children's Hospital - for believing me and validating my pain.

Mental Health and Psychology Support

Dr Elisabeth Hoehn and the team at Nundah CYMHS – for carrying me through my mental health journey from 2–13.

The team at Bayside CYMHS – for helping me through my phobias.

Anthea Burton and the team at Evolve Wellbeing – for helping me feel seen and held. Every time I walk out of your 'clinic' I feel like I've been wrapped in a big hug.

Business, Mentors, and Professional Support

Linda Enever from Enever Group – for encouraging me to write this book and for helping me from start to finish. Thank you so much to all the team for your help and for being incredible superstars.

Garry White and Rebecca – for encouraging me to start my business in the first place and for being the first people who believed in me in the outside community.

Sharron Pountney from SLP Consulting – for helping me register my companies and supporting me all these years, for believing in me, encouraging me and answering my questions. Thank you for making my dream come true.

Michelle Worthington - for helping me get started on my author journey.

Chris O Byrne and Kate Duncan for helping me with my children's picture book page designs. Thank you for being so helpful and believing in the power of my books.

Chloe Johnson and Tania Davidson for all your beautiful illustrations for Our Pixie Friends.

Max Perks, Ben, and the team at Rouken and Zipsites – for looking at and believing in my ideas even if they just looked like scribbles on a page. Thank you for building my website. Thank you Murray Paynter-Wiliams for phase two.

Ethan Donati and Cherie Eilertsen – for helping me feel more confident in my speaking journey. Without you, I would not be doing talks to 3,000 people or be where I am today.

Leanne Hardinge – for encouraging me to know my worth and never being afraid to say it how it is.

Kelly Dyer – for giving me so much valuable advice and believing in me.

Julie Bannister and the KBN Group – for all the learning and advice and for celebrating me for who I am.

Philippa Fisher – for never giving up on me and being so kind and patient with me.

The team at Redlands Coast Chamber of Commerce – for being my first business group and lowering your young entrepreneur age limit for me. Thank you for celebrating every win with me.

Scott Miller and team from BOP Industries, Taj Pabari and team from the ASE group, Young Changemakers and Enterprising Girls - for believing that young people can make a difference in the world.

Bill Blaikie – for helping me to write about the tough stuff and for sharing your PTSD journey with me.

All my sprizzletastic sponsors

Thank you to all my fantastic sponsors for helping me impact the lives of so many children. With your continued support, I can keep sprinkling pixie magic in our community: Mike Clark from Developing Australian Communities, the Forno brothers from Complete Insurance Advice, Lynne Sturgess from Precision Loans, Rotary Club of Capalaba, St Rita's Catholic Parish, Michelle Meurs from Shoebox Books, Knights of the Southern Cross, Cody and Leigh from DEC, Fairy Holly, Gift Packaging and Accessories, Ant Packaging and Planet-Friendly Packaging.

Thanks also to the Queensland Government in conjunction with the Redland City Council for the Regional Arts Development Fund grant which helped me publish *Minksy the Meltdown Pixie Helps Tommy* to help children with anxiety.

To everyone else who has helped me in my journey, thank you for believing in me.

Other Supports

Ryan Primer from youranxietyislying2yew – for saving my life more times than I can count.

Alex Warren, Cimorelli, Matthew West, Lauren Daigle, Lewis Capaldi, for KING AND COUNTRY, and Livingston – for supporting my mental health through your incredible music.

Molly Carlson – for showing me it's okay to cry and need support sometimes.

Joel, Luke, and Ollie – my incredible piggie pets.

And to you – for being so caring, compassionate, and open to hearing my story. I hope reading this book has helped you change the way you view trauma and inspire you to help as many kids as you can.

References

Cornoldi, C., Mammarella, I. C., Koster, M., & Semrud-Clikeman, M. (2022). Developmental visual-spatial disorder: Proposal for DSM-5 inclusion and critical review of current evidence. *Child Neuropsychology, 28*(3), 277–299. https://doi.org/10.1080/09297049.2021.1990674

Fine, J. G., Semrud-Clikeman, M., Bledsoe, J., & Musielak, K. A. (2013). A critical review of the literature on NLD as a diagnostic entity. *Child Neuropsychology, 19*(2), 190–223. https://doi.org/10.1080/09297049.2011.615351

Mammarella, I. C., & Cornoldi, C. (2014). An analysis of the criteria and cognitive profile of nonverbal learning disability. *Learning Disabilities Research & Practice, 29*(4), 173–181. https://doi.org/10.1111/ldrp.12040

Margolis, A. E., Pagliaccio, D., Langer, N., Marsh, R., & Posner, J. (2020). Neuroanatomical correlates of nonverbal learning disability: A preliminary investigation. *Journal of the International Neuropsychological Society, 26*(2), 127–137. https://doi.org/10.1017/S1355617719000843

Peterson, B. S., Kane, M. J., Alexander, K., & Margolis, A. E. (2021). Cerebellar white matter and social difficulties in children with nonverbal learning disability. *The Cerebellum, 20*(1), 100–113. https://doi.org/10.1007/s12311-020-01172-4

Rourke, B. P. (1989). *Nonverbal Learning Disabilities: The Syndrome and the Model.* Guilford Press.

Rourke, B. P. (1995). *Syndrome of Nonverbal Learning Disabilities: Neurodevelopmental Manifestations.* Guilford Press.

Rourke, B. P., & Tsatsanis, K. D. (2000). Nonverbal learning disabilities and Asperger syndrome. In A. Klin, F. R. Volkmar, & S. S. Sparrow (Eds.), *Asperger Syndrome* (pp. 231–258). Guilford Press.

Volden, J., & Sagvolden, T. (2011). Nonverbal learning disability: A disorder of right hemisphere development. *Developmental Medicine & Child Neurology, 53*(Suppl. 4), 46–51. https://doi.org/10.1111/j.1469-8749.2011.04055.x

www.ingramcontent.com/pod-product-compliance
Lightning Source LLC
Chambersburg PA
CBHW051420290426
44109CB00016B/1367